the beauty of
Success

FEATURING STORIES FROM THE TOP RATED PODCAST,
BUSINESS OF THE BEAT

the beauty of

Success

Start,
Grow,
and
Accelerate
Your Brand

KENDRA BRACKEN-FERGUSON

WILEY

For general information on our other products and services or for technical support, please contact
our Customer Care Department within the United States at (800) 762-2974, outside the United
States at (317) 572-3993 or fax (317) 572-4002.

Wiley also publishes its books in a variety of electronic formats. Some content that appears in print
may not be available in electronic formats. For more information about Wiley products, visit our web
site at www.wiley.com.

Library of Congress Cataloging-in-Publication Data is Available:

ISBN 9781394162949 (Cloth)
ISBN 9781394162987 (ePub)
ISBN 9781394162994 (ePDF)

COVER DESIGN: PAUL MCCARTHY

SKY10063170_122723

If you have ever thought about becoming an entrepreneur and finding your true defining life pillars to guide your journey, this book is for you.

With Immense Gratitude:

For my mother, Teresa Bledsoe, who taught me to love the Lord, treat people right, and do my best.

For my husband, Pleas Ferguson, who is my life partner and pushes me to value my extraordinary gifts and talent.

For my daughter, Tierra Ferguson, who gives me joy and something greater than myself and my work to cherish and love.

I support whatever decision you make because I truly believe that you have a heart for God and that you truly listen and seek His guidance. What He has in store for you is greater than you can ever imagine.

Make sure that the language of the agreement protects you and BrainTrust. Take care of your team. Do what is right—do your best and treat people right.

Carve out the things that are important to you and that are nonnegotiable.

T.

—Teresa Bledsoe (my mom), as written to me in 2018 when I was deciding on whether to go back into the world of being an entrepreneur

Contents

List of Podcast Excerpts

Listen to Kendra's podcast, *Business of the Beat*, wherever you listen to podcasts. *Business of the Beat* continues to be solely focused on the business of beauty and wellness specifically from the viewpoint of BIPOC founders, senior executives, and operators. The show focuses on the real stories of passion to profit where guests share the highs and lows, successes and learnings of launching, building, scaling, and exiting their companies. The show has more than 100 episodes across two seasons and kicked off season 3 on January 3, 2023.

We've included the following excerpts in the book.

Guest Name	Podcast Episode	Season/ Episode	Date First Aired	Chapter
Rachel Roff	Unlocking Inequalities for Darker Skin	Season 1, Episode 7	January 23, 2021	1
Angela Manuel Davis	Living in Purpose	Season 2, Episode 9	March 27, 2022	2

Guest Name	Podcast Episode	Season/ Episode	Date First Aired	Chapter
Youmie Francois	Creating a Money Mindset	Season 2, Episodes 42 and 43	November 13, 2022	2
Angel Cornelius	Lessons from the "Book of Failures"	Season 2, Episode 3	February 13, 2022	3
Dionne Phillips	I Said Yes to Everything	Season 1, Episode 46	October 24, 2021	4
Natasha Edwards	The Journey to Peace, Purpose, and Community	Season 2, Episode 16	May 15, 2022	5
Tai Beauchamp	Knowing When and How to Pivot	Season 1, Episode 35	August 8, 2021	5
Lisa Price	Pass It Forward	Season 1, Episode 18	April 11, 2021	6
Troy Alexander	An Extraordinary Story of Brand Manifestation	Season 2: Episode 11	April 10, 2022	6
Helen Aboah	We All Win Together	Season 2, Episode 13	April 24, 2022	6
Chidinma Asonye	Will vs. Skill	Season 1, Episode 19	April 18, 2021	7
Joni Odum	Keep Recreating What's Next	Season 2, Episode 41	November 6, 2022	8
Tonya Lewis Lee	Team Is Everything	Season 3, Episode 6	February 12, 2023	9
Charreah Jackson	Honoring Your Legacy	Season 1, Episode 9	February 6, 2021	9
Junior Mintt	I Choose Me Everyday	Season 2, Episode 25	July 17, 2022	9

Guest Name	Podcast Episode	Season/ Episode	Date First Aired	Chapter
Monaè Everett	Get Out of Your Own Way	Season 3: Episode 1	January 8, 2023	10
Nyakio Grieco	Nyakio Grieco	Season 1, Episode 1	December 12, 2020	11
Ron Robinson	There's Nothing Quite Like Beauty Products	Season 2, Episode 26	March 27, 2022	12

Foreword

Picture early fall on a crisp LA afternoon; I wore a dark green Italian wool double-breasted suit (lol). I'd heard *amazing* things about Kendra's impact and contributions but had yet to experience them first-hand until that night at Gwyneth's. I vividly recall how Kendra made me feel; she was completely engaged. I knew after one quick conversation with her that I'd know more about the life we were *meant* to live. I felt clear, more focused, and ready.

The moment Gwyneth thanked her guests and introduced Kendra to "take it away," my life changed. This incredible Black woman with strong, poised body language began to speak and shared with us what she knew we needed to do—what we needed to know! She was audibly arresting. The entire audience was in a trance, myself included. I wanted to know more about what seasons an individual in this way. What leads someone to champion people (our people) in this way? I wanted to be a student.

In Kendra's words:

One moment, one job, one career, or one person does not define your success. You must define what success looks like for you and what will enable you to live the highest expression of self that is so gratifying and rewarding while also realizing that your viewpoint will change with time and experience. People may try to erase you or change history, but ultimately they do not have that much power to erase the truth. Stand in your truth at all times.

Sometimes the path to intrapraneurship is parallel to entrepreneurship, as both are driven by an innate desire to create and build something.

This book is an ultra-modern blueprint for navigating the wilderness of entrepreneurship while sowing the seeds of self-reflection with an emphasis on *grace*. Kendra has a natural curiosity for what makes each intrapreneur and/or entrepreneur unique and the ability to engage the student in us all. We don't need permission to align and tap into our authentic selves, and Kendra's work and ideas are the perfect reminders.

It was refreshing and inspiring to read the stories and conversations of founders, entrepreneurs, and divine minds that serve as a guiding light for those of us who are blessed enough to hear them. These guidelines and this roadmap unite us *all* in a shared desire to live *in purpose, on purpose*.

Sir John Barnett
Makeup artist, activist, influencer, executive
January 2023

Preface:
An Invitation
to Freedom:
Unlocking the
Entrepreneurship
Journey

You are ready to be free and ask the hard questions to unlock that freedom. The only way to true freedom is to unlock and challenge the thing that has held you back. When you are ready, you are willing to do things that you wouldn't do before. And now you are willing to do things that you once were not ready to do.

—Julie Flanders (executive coach, mentor, and close friend), words spoken to me on September 1, 2022, during an executive coaching session

This is a divine season, and there is a divine energy surrounding this book. It is the journey, temerity, and tenacity that has taken me from intrapreneur to entrepreneur, back to intrapreneur, and ultimately living in my destiny as an entrepreneur. Throughout this journey, I have landed on the core pillars and truths that I know bring me freedom and ignite my path: **community**, **mentorship**, **education**, and **capital**.

To define each pillar separately would be to undervalue each of them; we must look at them as the sum of their parts and the source of my energy as a founder and voice in the world.

We are not meant to walk through life alone; we are meant to live in a **community** as a brain trust. According to the *Cambridge Dictionary*, a *brain trust* is a "group of people who advise a leader." For me, my brain trust is the core group of people I trust to collaborate, consult, and advise me in business. My ability to go from vision to execution is derived from the consistent presence of my brain trust. In fact, our overall personal happiness and pleasure may be derived from our internal ability to love, nurture, and care for ourselves, but that happiness is amplified and heightened when we have a community, or brain trust, of people we trust to go through the good times and the bad times. How boring would life be if we never heard other perspectives or never felt the emotional empathy of others?

I have learned some of my best lessons from **mentorship**. I am inspired to learn and want to give and receive knowledge. Being a mentor is a great responsibility and one that I cherish. When we allow ourselves to be both teacher and student, we open ourselves to the nuances that lateral relationships can never deliver. The greatest teachings reside in life experiences and individual approaches to living. Yes, there is a benefit to more experience—you'll have had more encounters, so there are more opportunities to grow. There is also a benefit to being a newcomer—the fresh, "bright-eyed bushy-tailed" outlook. I've been both mentor and mentee and am certain that they each provided different elements to my life just when I needed them most.

I chose the fastest path to a master's degree to get to my place as a professional in the world of business—I had deals to make, ladders to climb, and boardrooms to conquer. My lifelong friend Ebony Wilkins, who encouraged and coached me to write this book, has at least five degrees, and I have always admired her patience and approach to learning. She stayed her course, she fed her soul with knowledge, and I respect her so much for her own path to freedom. **Education** is a funny thing; you can truly never have too much of it because there is always something new to learn. Every year, I write "What do I need to learn this year?" to myself—2022 was the year of Web3, Blockchain, the Metaverse, and investing. I am still on an educational journey for the first three, and while now I can say that I am officially an investor and fund manager, I will never stop learning about investing and the venture space. For 2023, my goals are rooted around seeking equity and expanding economic advancement for Black founders through our BrainTrust Founders Studio. Equity is powerful and drives the most impact by recognizing that each person has different circumstances and allocates the exact resources and opportunities needed to reach an equal outcome. While these goals are lofty, every founder we support and investment we make takes us one step closer to accomplishing these goals on a daily basis. As I step out to be of service and do my life's work, I know I am walking on the shoulders of those who have opened doors and created spaces before me. It is all interconnected. The more we know, the more "woke" we are and the more we are encouraged to keep pushing forward. Education is also very personal—what is important to you to learn may not be important for me to learn. When we think about people having been denied education, it is the ultimate expression of repression and slavery in the most modern form. To be educated is to seek a level of freedom that only knowledge in new things can provide. You are free to learn, and you are free to grow in whatever area of your life is craving enrichment.

I believe that community begets mentorship, which creates pathways for education, which leads to monetary value; in other words, capital. **Capital** is defined as the most important or most serious relationship to wealth. In business and economics, the three most common types of capital are financial, human, and social. I look at all three as essential to maximizing this pillar for myself and my community. Defining and acquiring capital are parallel to community, mentorship, and education on the human level as well as the tactical nature of capital to run a business. At times I have lost balance and been focused on one pillar while losing sight of the others. It is that self-actualization of the connectivity of all four that is centering when it's rocky and that gives perspective on satisfaction, humility, and direction.

I am a founder in my bones and in my core. I am a visionary in my heart, and according to Genetic Matrix (an app-based software that provides human design and astrology charts and tools), I am an *emotional generator*, an opportunistic role model with a strategic personality who is motivated by hope and wanting. I was designed to survive. I am a theist, which, according to Merriam Webster, is one who believes in the existence of one God viewed as the creative source of the human race—which I do believe. Human design shows you where and how to access your body's consciousness as a decision-making tool and, ultimately, how to live as your true self.

I invite you to join me in my story of freedom and my unwavering servitude aligned with my core pillars of **community**, **mentorship**, **education**, and **capital**. I hope that you will find helpful nuggets from my story and experiences throughout this book, whether you are pursuing an entrepreneurial path or are an intrapreneur climbing the corporate ladder. Remember to discover your own guiding pillars, discover what ignites your passion, and hold tight to your brain trust.

As we go on this journey together, start with your own pillars. It doesn't matter how many you have; just write toward your own North Star.

What guiding principles are your compass as you navigate your professional journey?

_____

_____

_____

_____

_____

What words define how you show up armed for what lies ahead? How do you define each word?

_____

_____

_____

_____

_____

Throughout this book, I invite you to replace my pillars with your own and continue to expand on your *why* and purpose.

Carpe diem!

1

Are You an Entrepreneur or Intrapreneur?

Dear Kendra,

I THINK you ARE an entrepreneur learning for your OWN purposes and leadership the LESSONS that INTRAPRENEURSHIP offers you right now so that the NEXT TIME you put on the LEADER's ROBES, they will be higher quality fabric :-) and you will have ALL THE SUPPORT you need as the CHIEF AND CHAMPION of your projects to have a team of INTRAPRENEURS to EXECUTE.

—Love, Julie Flanders (my executive coach, as told to me in 2019 upon returning to entrepreneurship)

As an *intrapreneur*, I was calculated and political, and I prayed every day that I would have a seat at the table to do what I was hired to do for the company I worked for. I was an employee, a boss, and a leader, but I was undervalued.

As an *entrepreneur,* I took risks, I made decisions, I prayed every day we'd make payroll, but I was the bearer of all decisions, successes, and failures. I was a chief and my own champion, mentor, colleague, and coach. Entrepreneurs and visionaries encompass a much smaller group than what is portrayed by job titles; there are a lot of people who pretend or wish. Entrepreneurs see possibilities that other people can't.

Having spent the past 20 years of my career navigating between my role as an intrapreneur and my role as an entrepreneur, I have created a set of definitions that I believe summarize both.

1. *Intrapreneurs* are internal corporate entrepreneurs who follow the goals of the organization.
2. *Entrepreneurs* follow their dreams and passions. They aren't confined to the goals of a company or bound by the hierarchy, the politics, or the boundaries that intrapreneurs face.

The qualities that make good intraprenuers and good entrepreneurs exist in both people, and sometimes the path to intrapreneurship is parallel to entrepreneurship, as both are driven by an innate desire to create and build something. This chapter takes you on my journey from entrepreneur to intrapreneur to entrepreneur again. My hope is that it will help guide your path to embrace which direction is right for you: maybe it's a mix of both and maybe, like me, you will go between the two throughout your journey to ignite and fuel your passions, aspirations, and purpose.

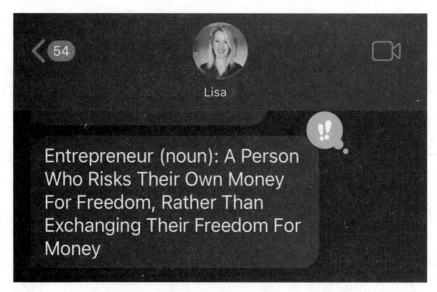

Text message from Lisa Stone, co-founder and chief investment officer, BrainTrust Founders Studio

Intrapreneur versus Entrepreneur

> Entrepreneurship is very romanticized.
>
> —Samantha Golay, HR executive
> recruiter, Netflix

Not everyone aspires or wants to become an entrepreneur. Some businesspeople are content to lead teams and manage employees but don't want to take on the risk or financial responsibility of being an entrepreneur.

According to Ebrary.net, "Moreover, although there are probably tens of millions of potential entrepreneurs in the United States alone, most people simply are not in a position to pursue their entrepreneurial dreams and ideas for a variety of reasons, including financial constraints, family concerns, and others."

Intrapreneurs have the safety net of a company, are able to lead a team, and have a voice and opinion, but, ultimately, final company decisions are not solely in their hands. Senior management will listen and support, but an intrapreneur's paycheck doesn't necessarily stop if their ideas get nixed. Intrapreneurs are ambassadors of other chiefs' or leaders' ideas, vision, and direction who ultimately look to others for final buy-in and approval.

By definition, intrapreneurship is the act of behaving like an entrepreneur while working within a large organization. According to "Intra-Corporate Entrepreneurship" by Gifford Pinchot III and Elizabeth S. Pinchot, the first written use of the terms *intrapreneur, intrapreneuring,* and *intrapreneurship* date from a 1978 paper. The term *intrapreneurship* was used in the popular media first in February 1985 in the *TIME* magazine article "Here Come the Intrapreneurs" by John S. Demott and then later in the same year in *Newsweek,* when Steve Jobs, Apple Computer's chairman, was quoted as saying, "The Macintosh team was what is commonly known as intrapreneurship; only a few years before the term was coined—a group of people going, in essence, back to the garage, but in a large company."

For me, I had to grow and expand my career through experiencing both professional paths, starting as an intrapraneur, taking the leap as an entrepreneur, resolving to go back to being an intrapraneur, and ultimately claiming my lifelong destiny as an entrepreneur. I had to address my natural sense of individuality, vision, and creativity, and what I learned is that it was important to be honest with myself about how I wanted to show up in the world. I had to embrace and walk confidently in my resolve that I am an entrepreneur and there is no amount of money or fame that can change that. I realized that I let people's opinions of fancy titles, company size, and status influence my decision and redefine what was important for me. Not only did this hurt me in some situations, but it also impacted those around me. Deciding what is important while also balancing personality factors and life situations is key. Your intuition is strong. Trust it. I am sharing my journey of how I learned to navigate wearing both hats in the hopes that you'll take what you need and be encouraged to create your own path.

My Journey from Entrepreneur to Intrapreneur to Entrepreneur Again

As I mentioned, I have been both entrepreneur and intrapreneur at various stages of my life. Traveling this journey back and forth has given me unique insight into the differences between them and how one or the other will talk to your soul.

I started my career in the community relations department at the Indiana Pacers in 2000. From there I took a position in New York to become an assistant account executive at FleishmanHillard (FH), one of the largest public relations agencies in the world. After helping build the digital practice group at FH and becoming one of the youngest vice presidents in the company, I was recruited by Ralph Lauren to become their first director of digital media, launching the first global influencer campaigns and the brand across social media. At both FH and Ralph Lauren, I was an intrapreneur creating a new division, a new capability, and new revenue streams for the company.

When I was 29, I became an entrepreneur by starting my first company, Digital Brand Architects (DBA), one of the first talent management agencies for bloggers. It was at DBA that I had my first experience raising money and earned the distinction of being one of the first 100 Black women to raise more than $1 million for her company.

From there, in January 2015, I continued feeding my entrepreneurial spirit and went on to found BrainTrust, a brand development, social media, and influencer marketing agency that drives brand strategy and builds products and online communities for celebrities and global brands.

In 2017, I decided to take a lucrative offer and what I thought was all the risk off my plate when I allowed Creative Artists Agency–Global Brands Group (CAA-GBG) to acquire BrainTrust. Now, instead of being the founder, I was answering to others as the chief digital officer. Back to being an intrapreneur. Then, in an interesting turn of events, I bought BrainTrust back in 2019 and expanded the agency in 2021 to launch BrainTrust Founders Studio, now the largest membership-based platform dedicated to Black founders of beauty and wellness companies. Further building the BrainTrust ecosystem, in 2022 I co-founded BrainTrust Fund, our first venture fund to invest capital in Black-founded beauty and wellness companies.

Now, as a founder three times over, I understand and recognize that, ultimately, the deal I made as an entrepreneur to become an intrapreneur was not the deal I would have made as an intrapreneur to become an entrepreneur. I confused mentorship for definitive direction and followed negative advice such as "You are better off without the headache of running your own business" and "You don't have the systems in place to compete" to heart.

The responsibility faced by entrepreneurs as the captain of the ship means balancing a personal affinity for the team and the business with the practicality of running a business and being accountable for the livelihoods of that team. For me, I didn't want to be a "solopreneur" running a business; I wanted multiple teams, breadth across different geographical markets, and the ability to grow and scale across different industries. I was taking the path of least resistance when I left entrepreneurship to become an intrapreneur. Let's face it, I was simply tired and was overexposed to other people's success as a metric for my own.

When I think about my path of leaving entrepreneurship to go back to intrapreneurship, I later realized that I allowed the wrong feedback to seep into my consciousness. The negative feedback was not rooted in the education of the path either as an intrapreneur or entrepreneur but was the catalyst of fear that at times I transferred to others in ways that diminished my value.

Don't get me wrong. There were many upsides to being an intrapreneur. It truly took some pressure off of me financially because, as an entrepreneur, I was responsible for so many people, financial commitments, and operational tasks to make the business run. Intrapreneurship took me inside a global company, generated personal press, positioned me on the scene and radar of peers and colleagues, and created the perception that was the reality of a "come up." I expanded my team, built a base of clients, and strengthened my internal database of contacts and networks. As an intrapreneur, I had a kind of financial support and security that only a global company can provide.

I had an expense account, a fancy office in an even fancier building, and newfound access. I wasn't worried about payroll and rent; I was worried about fitting in, making numbers, reporting, and relearning how to be a good employee and reporting to a manager or, in corporate-speak, "managing up"—a task I utterly loathe.

The *Harvard Business Review* defines "managing up" as "Being the most effective employee you can be, creating value for your boss and your company." It wasn't that I didn't want to learn how to "communicate effectively" with my boss or learn his management, leadership, and communication style; it was more that I wanted to get the work done, be the best at the work, and plow forward in my own style. For me, the experience was humbling, psychologically damaging, and riddled with myriad stereotypes of corporate personalities that came to life before my eyes. That's why it's important to align your own vision, passions, and direction for your career with the right decision that will propel you to greatness. For me, that meant understanding the right fit at different pressure points in my career. It's not just about surviving; it's about thriving and understanding when you've hit a roadblock or a glorious mountain to climb.

It's easy to explain why I took the in-house position at CAA-GBG after being out on my own. Ever since I had started my first company, I secretly deep down wanted to work at CAA—mainly because of the intrigue and the perception of being at the top. It was the same reason I ended up working at the global PR firm FleishmanHillard too; they were number 1 and at the top. I strive to sit on top of the mountain, not live in the valley. I had a vision early on in my professional career and CAA sat prominently on my vision board for many years. I was able to manifest that vision at 2000 Avenue of the Stars in Los Angeles.

Brandon Carter, managing partner of BrainTrust, and Kendra Bracken-Ferguson, moving into CAA on November 15, 2017

In that building, I got a taste of the physical corporate notion I thought I wanted—the address, the office, the view. I met some good and not so good people but learned so many lessons coming out of the experience. From my experience as an intrapreneur, I was able to apply those lessons in my life, redefine how I wanted to do business, sharpen what I wanted out of business, and home in on the type of work I excel at and how to build the bridge to my next blessing.

Tips for Surviving as an Intrapreneur

- When someone asks to "pick your brain" and they are your boss, make sure they aren't claiming your ideas, thoughts, or work as their own. The characteristics of a good boss are to give you credit for your work and for them to feel proud that they identified you as a core member of their team versus being threatened by your greatness.
- Stand up for yourself. In many companies, there is an HR function or senior person to talk to when a situation doesn't feel right; always speak up and do it in a way that is not immediately accusatory or aggressive. We sometimes go into a situation with our fists up and ready to box; your approach and positioning in every situation will fundamentally shape the outcome.
- Do not allow anyone to change who you are. If someone has so much control over you that your ethics are compromised, figure out the fastest way to exit.
- Approach the situation with the best outcome that can happen in your mind; in other words, stay positive. Your attitude in those first 90 days will determine how you perform overall. It will lay the foundation for how you show up and how people perceive you.

I hit my roadblock as an intrapreneur under the corporate structure when a senior executive told me he didn't see color after I questioned why I wasn't being leveraged as the first chief digital officer and only Black female officer in the company.

"When you 'claim' to not see a person's race, you are denying the very fabric of their being. You are denying

something that they cannot and should not 'rid' or deny themselves of. How can we deny in others what they cannot and should not deny in themselves? A student cannot not see their race. It looks them in the face every day as they look in the mirror. Their race contributes to the experiences that they have as they navigate through society."
—Makeda Brome, an instructional math coach at Fort Pierce Westwood Academy in Fort Pierce, Florida

It wasn't just my managers denying who I was that made me want to get out from under the corporate structure. It was also the acts of sabotage on a daily basis, such as being told by senior leadership that the rug color in my office didn't match company policy after I met all of my performance goals for that quarter or that one woman was enough representation in a new business meeting when I asked why I wasn't included given my expertise in the area. I learned that discrimination is alive and omnipresent in corporate structures, especially toward women of color, and I had reached a point where working for others was not for me in the role of employee.

My boss and I reached the end of the road after months of discussions, debates, and trying to determine the best course forward. I will say—and I truly believe—that he always had the best intention for our partnership. He and I are both visionaries, and to this day, I will thank him for believing in me and taking a chance on BrainTrust. During this time, I had many choices to make, and I chose to recommit to myself and my team as a founder and CEO.

In May 2019, my relationship with CAA–GBG ended. After two years of being an intrapreneur, I ventured out on my own again. I bought back BrainTrust, and my team and I were once again out in the wild. It was hard, it was emotional, and it was a time of deep reflection: What did I do wrong? What could I have done better? Was I doomed from the beginning? Who really had my back? My soft landing came from my longtime friend and collaborator Moj Mahdara, who told me to bring my team and work from their office, and she would help me rebuild my company. One step in front of the other, one day at a time, and with a dedicated team who packed up our fancy office at 2000 Avenue of the Stars, we dove headfirst back into "startup" territory with a few boxes, a roster of great clients, and something to prove.

"Entrepreneurism is the most beautiful paintbrush one can have."
—Moj Mahdara, managing partner/co-founder
of Kinship Ventures, co-founder and
chair of the board of BeautyUnited,
and guest on Season 1, Episode 50 of
Business of the Beat podcast

At that time of my life, I did not see my pillars—community, mentorship, education, and capital—as connected yet. They existed in a siloed expression of what was important to me: building new things, being of service to others, sharing my knowledge and expertise, and finding new opportunities to learn and grow. For me, the only way to truly be educated was to step out in faith and navigate the course of my career back as an entrepreneur.

An Entrepreneur for Sure

In 2019 the BrainTrust agency was consciously uncoupling with CAA–GBG and becoming independent again. During this time, I was working hard as an entrepreneur to rebuild the agency, working as a business partner to an A-list celebrity to build her health and wellness brand, as well as just living my regular life as a mom, wife, daughter, and friend.

With BrainTrust being independent once again, we dove headfirst into what we called BrainTrust 3.0, developing our core pillars as an agency, rebuilding our revenue, and toeing the line between our old business model and innovating into a new agency model. We were riding high, generating new clients, and leveraging our new relationship with Beautycon, the largest beauty festival in the United States.

As part of this, I became a shareholder in Beautycon and took the title of chief business officer. To this day, I believe that Beautycon was one of the most important movements in the beauty industry. Walking into the Beautycon festival was a surreal experience. It was the Super Bowl of the beauty industry, complete with glitter, more makeup samples in one room than any Target or Ulta, and an energy of acceptance, realness, and a melting pot of brand executives, influencers, beauty lovers, celebrities, and product junkies all in one room convening around the magic of beauty uniting people across racial, gender, and class lines.

This was a special time and one that pushed my wherewithal and faith to levels I had not experienced. I was once again wearing my intrapreneurial hat, but this time simultaneously while acting as an entrepreneur. The plurality of these roles is not something I would wish on any one person. It's hard enough to do one really well but to be both and do both was not sustainable for any of us. It's a pattern of excess that, through deep self-actualization and awareness, I have learned to steer away from.

The gift of March 2020 for me was that it was a forced outlet to stop living a dual life and make a choice. I chose BrainTrust as an entrepreneur and never looked back.

Settling into Entrepreneurism: Pivoting Through COVID and Making Mistakes

2020 hit us all hard. It was a surreal moment for so many people, and it was during this time that the four pillars of community, mentorship, education, and capital that subconsciously ruled my view of business started to align in a powerful way. It was during this time that I fought, struggled, and did my best to power myself and my team through such a significant loss of revenue that our only lifeline was receiving paycheck protection program (PPP) loans and financing. I will never forget getting that approval letter from Elizabeth Horton, my longtime finance partner, that we had been approved for a loan. There are moments in life where you know exactly where you were, what you were doing, and the feelings that ensued. I don't remember much from the early days of the pandemic, but this memory in the form of a PPP lifeline for me, my team, my family, and my company is clear.

After that moment, I pivoted the business to dive into a partnership with a company based in Israel that in my mind was the best way to get through the pandemic, as about 70% of our revenue was derived from our digitally activated events business and on-site get-togethers that were no longer taking place. I was seeking a community to help us generate revenue, but as we dove deeper into that partnership, I became unsettled and highly cautious. I knew something was off, and I couldn't figure out how to navigate around that feeling. I learned a lot about rushing into that partnership: when your back is against the wall as an entrepreneur, survival mode kicks in, and the choices you make are not always the same choices you make in times of abundance and growth.

It took courage to admit that the partnership I thought would be the pivot of our business was not the right direction for the company. We spent the early days of the COVID pandemic on a hamster wheel, with countless hours on Zoom meetings, trying to appease our new partners and save the company.

I read something in my horoscope on Co-Star, an astrological social networking service, that spoke to this and sat so deeply in my heart: "Your main challenge right now is to change up the structures in your life. You don't have to stop having relationships, but you do have to stop thinking about people as a way out."

I didn't spend the months of lockdown during the COVID pandemic in self-reflection mode like many people did. The year 2020 was one of the busiest, most challenging times of my professional career. It was the moment when I was either going to self-destruct or make it to the other side stronger. And as I reshaped my circumstances to leverage my community, reconnect with my executive coach for mentorship, and determine how to educate myself into the next version of myself and career, I prayed that we would be alright, like Kendrick Lamar says in "Alright" on his 2015 album *To Pimp a Butterfly*: "If God got us then we gon' be alright," which ultimately became my anthem, theme song, and motivator to keep going.

What song, lyric, poem, or quote motivates you?

_____

_____

_____

_____

_____

Are you smiling? Are you ready to conquer your greatest fears? Is your heart beating fast? How do the words make you feel in your core?

_____

_____

_____

_____

_____

Why do these words motivate you?

_____

_____

_____

_____

Fully Embracing Entrepreneurism: Hosting a Podcast and Highlighting Leaders

Armed with the notion that we were going to be alright, in 2020 I was approached by Celessa Baker, Vice President Brand Marketing, Makeup & Haircare at SEPHORA, to host a beauty podcast. Celessa and I met during a photo shoot for *Essence* magazine when we were both named in their "17 Inspiring Black Executives Redefining the Face of Beauty" and were featured on the April digital cover and in print.

March/April 2020 Essence Magazine Digital Cover behind the scenes glam.
From Right: Kendra Bracken-Ferguson, Teresa Bledsoe, mom Jessica Santoni, long time makeup artist

After several conversations with the executive producer, Kenneth Johnson, and my alignment with his vision to create Mean Ole Lion Media as a Black-owned podcast network, featuring all Black hosts, I knew I had to say yes. It was this decision that would further unlock my pillars of mentorship and education to guide me in understanding and sharing entrepreneurism from the first-hand vantage point of multiple lived experiences from entrepreneurs across all walks of life. On December 12, 2020, we launched our first episode of *Business of the Beat*.

Business of the Beat is an innovative podcast designed to celebrate and share stories from diverse beauty and wellness founders and executives about their journey of launching, building, scaling, and growing their businesses. Leveraging my personal pillars of community, mentorship, education, and capital, each episode explores what it takes to build a sustainable brand with the goal of encouraging and creating a path for the next generation of diverse entrepreneurs and intrapreneurs.

> **Absolutely most inspiring podcast**   1y ago
> ★★★★★   Selflove88!
>
> I absolutely love this podcast! So inspirational!! As an entrepreneur in the beauty space I have learned so much from each founder as well as Kendra's journey! Thank you for creating such an amazing space Kendra!🖤

Through the podcast and this educational journey of learning and listening, I have had more than 120 conversations with both entrepreneurs and intrapreneurs. Whether you have decided you are an entrepreneur or an intrapreneur, at the end of the day, you must believe deeply in the path you have created for yourself. All lived experiences add up to the sum of the opportunity and decision you ultimately make to move in the right direction for you.

Having Passion as an Entrepreneur

When we think of building a successful business, a fulfilling life, and an abundant career, it is a simple equation: preparedness + opportunity = a tangible outcome that comes in the form of a service, a product, a brand, or an initiative. Then we get to the question of whether this outcome is fulfilling your desire and passion.

> "To build something from the ground up, you have to have undying passion for it."
>
> —Rachel Roff

One of my early conversations on *Business of the Beat* was with Rachel Roff, CEO and founder of Urban Skin Rx. Rachel is the epitome of leaning in and supporting her community, being a mentor to help ease the path for the next generation of leaders, understanding the importance of education through her unwavering journey to educate herself in an area that many were not exploring, and creating generational wealth for her daughter through a significant investment of her business. And she did it all with an unwavering passion to never take no for an answer. It was that passion that inspired me to eventually join the board of Urban Skin Rx.

Business of the Beat Excerpt, in Conversation with Rachel Roff

Season 1, Episode 7, January 23, 2021

edited for print

Kendra: You mentioned something that I think is why you've been so successful: you came up with an opportunity. You fulfilled a need, in particular for darker skin tones, for Brown and Black people and people of color, and your journey and your story are just amazing. So take us back: tell us how we got to these amazing products—our pillpads and our masks and everything that makes Urban Skin Rx so special.

Rachel: It was a long journey. I am not one of these founders that blew up after two years. I have been doing this for a long time. This July will be 15 years. I opened my medical spa (med spot) in Charlotte in 2006 [which I actually recently sold in September 2021] and started the skincare line 10 years ago. So I'm truly an OG at this point.

So my journey started, gosh, like 25 years ago; I grew up in Northern California in a pretty diverse, liberal Jewish family. We had a lot of diversity with our family, which I didn't really notice because it was just my family and my norm, and at a young age, I had a lot of skin problems from a precancerous mole on my face that led me to be very self-conscious. It was like a big chocolate spot that kids never let me forget was there, and then I ended up very overweight, about 60 pounds overweight, and ended up with acne as well.

I just felt horrible in the skin that I was in, and through being taken to dermatologists who happened to have estheticians on staff (because California was a little bit ahead of the time with med spots), I immediately knew this is what I want to do. It was like I want a profession where I can be around all the things that I can use on myself to make myself look better. But I also have always been somebody who's very empathetic, who really hated seeing any underdog or anybody who wasn't being treated equally.

Fast-forward to when I moved to Charlotte, North Carolina, and ended up going to esthetician school after college. Charlotte has got a very large ethnic community.

(continued)

It's pretty much 50% African American almost. And when I went into school, I very quickly noticed that it didn't represent the diversity within my town. It was a very Caucasian industry. Immediately, we were concentrating on skin conditions that really were typical of lighter skin tones, not ethnic skin. And when I brought in my family and friends to practice on (because you needed to do so to get all your credit), it wasn't necessarily like they were treated rudely. It was just like, "Don't do this and don't do that, because their skin is so sensitive, and I don't want you to burn them."

There's got to be a solution other than just massaging their face to make them feel good. We can make impacts in their lives. This really led me to have to pursue my own education, even down to ordering dermatology books for ethnic skin off of the Internet; seeking out continuing education courses, like in Atlanta around skin pigmentation and skin of color; and even through my first job as an esthetician, the guy happened to buy a laser that was safe for deeper skin tones, and he didn't even know it.

It was like, I don't have the strongest relationship with God. I'm not the most religious, but I'm a believer in God. And sometimes I look back on all the things that happened to me. From being bullied to ending up at this first job with this laser that happened to be for deeper skin tones and being trained in this laser and starting to practice on some of my friends. We ended up with the most amazing before and after pictures of this Black male friend of mine with ingrown hairs on his neck. This is such an amazing picture. Where are all the black men who could use this service? They're at the barber shop. So I hit the pavement in Charlotte and ended up going to, like, 50 barbershops. Walking into barber shops as a woman and distributing these flyers of before and after pictures is very intimidating.

It ended up working, and the doctor owned it and said, "What else can we do? You're so smart." I was like, "Well, I think we should go on the radio and say we have a laser hair removal device that works on deeper skin tones." And so I actually wrote the commercial. I will never forget; it said: "Ladies, are you tired of plucking those annoying chin hairs?" And it was like the phone just blew up. And so at the time, I was, like, 23, and I always wanted to open my own med spot, but I thought it would happen after five or 10 years of being in the game learning, and I just really felt like it was my calling.

I was so scared that somebody else would pursue this. I looked and saw that there were really no other med spas in the area and almost in the country specializing in deeper skin tones. So urgently, I went to my parents and was like, "Can you guys help me?" I always like to be transparent about that. My parents co-signed on a loan for me, and I know that was a huge blessing and advantage that not everybody has. I mean, the loan was in my name, but I did not have any substantial credit history or established income, and so I would not be here today if it wasn't for them. But I wrote this business plan with a bookkeeper and an accountant to kind of cross-reference numbers and make sure we were asking for a loan that would help us sustain. And I opened this very small med spot, and it boomed.

The interesting but terrible thing about it is, I would say, that up until maybe a year ago, I did not start having

(continued)

competition. And we can talk about that today, but literally, other than Ambi, I have been one of the only clinical skincare brands for deeper skin tones. And I felt so urgent 15 years ago, like, oh my God, any second now, somebody's going to launch, and I'm so excited that now I'm not the only one in the category. I feel really good that I can be successful with a lot of other people playing in the category.

I feel very proud that my success has made a lot of retailers want to pursue other brands and other brands have seen what I have done and it has led them to want to play in this category because they see my success, and it's so necessary.

But in terms of creating the skincare line, it came about after about four years of being an esthetician and med spa owner because there was no other skincare brand that really was catering to hyperpigmentation the way I wanted it to. And hyperpigmentation, which is uneven skin tone/dark spots, can affect everybody. I'm not African American, I'm not brown skin, but I suffer from hyperpigmentation. But it is more common with deeper skin tones. And so that is really what Urban Skin Rx is all about as a melanin expert; it's really about being an expert in the treatment of melanin, which we all have. But that's how we got here today.

Kendra: As a mentor, what do you want the next generation to take away from your experience as an entrepreneur and founder?

I think if there was a takeaway, one thing that I just love about this is giving somebody the gift of not making the mistakes I made. I do think that you can actually have a very successful business in two to three years. It doesn't have to take 10 to 15 years if you avoid a lot of the mistakes that I've made. Being able to pass those learning lessons forward is just so exciting for me. But I don't know, I think that there's just so many people who want to be a business owner because it's cool. And one, I do think that you really have to weigh out the questions and negatives because it's something that just never turns off. It's like getting married; to undo it is just so big.

But I think in terms of really being a founder from the ground up, you have to have an undying passion for something particular because that is the only thing that has gotten me through all the emotional and physical hardships and long hours. I mean, I think I will easily die 10 years early due to the inflammation in my body from stress. But I just want people to have passion. It really has to come from the right place; it can't just be to look cool.

It has to really change lives or to fill a need that affects you or your family or somebody you love. I really recommend strong passion.

Not only does Rachel share her journey of being an entrepreneur, but she talks about the really special moment when she was an intrapreneur working for someone else but had to find her own clients to create a path to generate commissions. She worked hard and leveraged her community by going into barber shops and educating her own clients to evangelize the brand, and it paid off. It was that journey as an intrapreneur first that led her to create the med spa, which led to a skincare line and her own incredible journey to entrepreneurship.

When I think of what I learned during my entrepreneurial journey, it is echoed by the lessons in my conversation with Rachel:

- A strong passion will hold you together when it's hard and you want to quit.
- Be open to following the path that others have turned away from or tried to persuade you wasn't for you; there is a reason you were called to travel the lonely road of discovery.
- Education is the root of expansion; it can come in many forms, even when you least expect it. Seek education at all costs. It's one of my four core pillars (community, mentorship, **education**, and capital) that has served me in moments of pivots and growth.
- Share insights, share feedback, and share knowledge with anyone who will listen and ask for the same in return; be ready to let your guard down, take what you need, and leave the rest behind.
- Support the decision that truly matches your personal path to fulfillment and follow your dreams like Rachel did from a spa to a product and beyond.

And always know that . . . "We gon' be alright!"

2 | Heart for God

You have to be careful not to allow people to dictate how you
feel about the circumstances of your life or your mere existence.
—Teresa Bledsoe, my mom

When I first moved to Los Angeles in 2014, I was stopped at a
red light less than a mile from my house for what seemed like an
eternity. My heart raced, and I remember tapping and tapping
on the steering wheel. I had an intense headache that was radiating across my forehead and a sharp pain in my chest. Was I
having a heart attack? Was I about to faint?

I later realized that I was reacting to being at a crossroads of
whether to stay or go in the first company I co-created, Digital
Brand Architects (DBA). I wanted to stay, but I also had a strong
desire to leave and start something new. This all came from a
division between me and my co-founders that was fueled by
ego, power, and a dynamic between three people that can only
come about in intense business relationships.

We had fundamentally different views. I remember one of
my partners saying she wanted to be a cult leader, which I later

understood to mean that she wanted to be the only person in charge and of authority. She wanted to control all aspects of the company and team and later created a false narrative that she was the founder of DBA. She tried to completely erase me from the company's history and creation story, when in truth, she was not at the kitchen table when Karen Robinovitz and I started DBA, nor was she present when we had the idea to launch and sign our first clients.

When Karen and I first hired her as our third partner, I immediately felt a putter-putter in my gut that I ignored. I lacked confidence and experience as a co-founder and operator and to that point had never been in a tug of war fueled by an absolute lack of trust and alignment with people I admired and truly cared for.

I am not good at manipulation. In the end, my co-founders and I simply did not agree, identify with each other, or align on the direction of the business. There was no connectivity on decisions being made about the business, and I was not consciously aware or experienced enough to play their game of chess. I did not yet have the confidence or trust in myself that I do today. I could not see how to get out and get to the other side; I felt trapped and that my entire career was riding on that one company and was my only way to reach success.

Two conversations happened, one with my longtime friend, Kathryn Finney, who is the founder and managing partner of Genius Guild, author of *Build the Damn Thing*, an internationally acclaimed speaker and award-winning executive. She sat with me in my backyard as I was going through this difficult period with DBA, and she said, "Sometimes it's okay to outgrow things or leave things that you started." Those words were so simple but pivotal at that time.

The second conversation was internal. I heard God say, "I wouldn't bring you here for you to fail." It was like a voice saying to me, "Straighten up and get it together; you won't fail in whatever you decide to do because I will never leave you nor forsake you." It was my heart for God that carried me through the difficult decision to leave DBA and start a new adventure.

> "Stop imitating the ideas and opinions of the culture around you, but be inwardly transformed by the Holy Spirit through a total reformation of how you think. This will empower you to discern God's will as you live a beautiful life, satisfying and perfect in his eyes."
> —Romans 12:2 TPT

The best lesson I learned from this experience was to believe in your dogma and stay true to a higher power, being, spirit, or ideology that is greater than you. Don't let anyone steal your joy and take you away from who you are. No one should have that much control over you, your health, and your decisions. When they do, you must take the hard step to leave, going deep into who you are and what you stand for, and reclaim your joy.

Building confidence is hard; what I also learned navigating the relationship and the divide between me and my co-founders at DBA was what I'm good at—building brands, developing cohesive strategies, connecting the dots, creating high-performing teams, and supporting not just my vision but the vision of others—as well as pushing myself to truly grasp what I'm capable of overcoming. For me, that means having a "heart for God" in all that I do and every moment of every day. One moment, one job, one career, or one person does not define your success; just like the idea of the path and company that I left behind. You must define what success looks like for you and what will enable you to live the highest expression of self that is soul-gratifying and rewarding, while also realizing that your viewpoint will change with time and experience. People may try to erase you or change history, but ultimately they do not have that much power. Stand in your truth at all times.

There were greater life lessons through my experience with DBA that I will always be thankful for:

1. Always speak up and trust myself, my gut, my ignition, and that putt-putt that is meant to make me take another clarifying look at my decisions and actions.
2. Speak on what I am good at and say it boldly and proudly. I will not leave the narrative of my core strengths in the hands of someone else to value or speak on.
3. Maintain my integrity at all costs; some people won't understand, and that's okay.
4. Claim ownership of my ideas and my intellectual property so my legacy is not lost, erased, or stolen.

Despite our strained relationship, DBA was widely successful. We were one of the first agencies to manage bloggers as talent and went on to manage some of the biggest influencers developing brands, products, TV shows, and book deals. We paved the way for the influencer management agencies that exist today. I credit all our partners with continuing the work that Karen and I started at Karen's kitchen table in 2010 to create a new blogger economy, which led to a collective reach of more than 200 million upon being acquired by United Talent Artist Agency (UTA). To this day, I will be proud of what all the founders and partners created and the work we did together to generate opportunities for the voices that became the face of our generation.

When I think about that five-year journey and all we accomplished at DBA, I celebrate all the wins, big and small. For some, success may be giving a big presentation, getting a new client, accomplishing a big project, or even just making payroll every month to keep pushing through. For some of us, success is being able to show up authentically in all of our glory at work. This is also one of the drivers for people starting their own businesses: they want the freedom to be who they are and live a purposeful life on their own terms.

Living in Purpose to Achieve the Highest Expression of Self

Who is Angela Manuel Davis? When I talked to her on my *Business of the Beat* podcast, Angela described herself as a child of God, a mother, a wife, a sister, and a coach. Overall, she is an encourager.

The world knows her as a five-time All-American member of the USA Track and Field team, an Olympic Trials semi-finalist, a member of the World Championship team, and a professional runner for Nike. She is also the beloved entrepreneur and highly inspiring co-founder and chief motivation officer of AARMY, a popular fitness app with on-demand exercise classes.

Besides leading the most sought-after group cycle class in Los Angeles, she has privately coached Beyoncé, Jay-Z, David Beckham, and Kerry Washington. Her positive message on living on purpose to achieve the highest expression of ourselves reverberates globally, amplified by her appearances during Oprah's Winfrey's Live the Life You Want Tour and Oprah's 20/20 Vision Tour.

She says, "Coming from a sports family and being a professional athlete myself, it's the marriage between sports and spirituality where I found my pocket . . . my sweet spot. I coach individuals to their best life using spiritual principles, but also using physicality."

Business of the Beat Excerpt, in Conversation with Angela Manuel Davis

Season 2, Episode 9, March 27, 2022

edited for print

Kendra Bracken-Ferguson
Business of the Beat Host

Angela Manuel Davis
Co-Founder of AARMY

Kendra: Angela Manuel Davis, who are you, and what do you stand for?

Angela: I'm a child of God. I am somebody who has dedicated my life to living in purpose and to encouraging everyone else around me to do the same. I'm a mom and a wife, a sister, a friend, a coach. And, you know, for me, when I look back at my life, the through line has been that of being an encourager. Coming from a sports family and being a professional athlete myself, it's the marriage between sport and spirituality where I found my pocket . . . my sweet spot. I coach individuals to their best life using spiritual principles, but also using physicality. There's something that's so beautiful that happens when we are in a place of vulnerability.

If we can all understand that every single one of us was created in purpose, on purpose, for a purpose, that means there is something that we were created to do in this world. We weren't created to find purpose because purpose was never lost. We were actually created with purpose, right? So discovering that for a lot of people is a journey all in itself. And imagine this: imagine if our bodies are what house our gifts and talents.

Kendra: You may be trying to figure out how your purpose shows up for you. But you intentionally have a purpose that's been placed upon your life, and that's how we weave our lives together. What have you been pouring into yourself to maintain that purpose and energy you pour into so many people as an encourager?

Angela: I think we share a lot of similarity in the sense that the first thing I do when I open my eyes is I say thank

(continued)

you. It's not rushing to my phone to check my messages and my emails, but it's spending time with the one that woke me up this morning, because not everybody was on the wake-up list. And the fact that I can open my eyes and be alive, that's gratitude. So I think about prayer and gratitude, and I feel like I am more efficient when I ground and anchor myself in prayer and gratitude at the top of the day.

But my mom and dad were really mindful. They would always say "garbage in, garbage out." And they would say "you need to protect your eye gates and your ear gates." So what we would play in our home would be things that would seep into us, unbeknownst to us as kids, and I feel like I've held onto that. I feel like that's how I stay fed; I'm constantly engaging in things that I know will nourish me spiritually so that I can do my life's work.

Earning and Claiming Ownership

Kendra: What does AARMY mean to you?

Angela: AARMY for me is my first business. I got to a point in my life where I knew that I had earned ownership. I had earned that right. I had earned the right to be an owner.

I'd earned that, and I took a leap of faith at a significant height in my career, but it was in my career as an employee, and I knew that was no longer what was for me. And I thought that for a really long time. To be honest with you, life was really good, and I didn't have to worry about who was paying the light bill and who was cleaning the toilets. I was crushing it, and I didn't have the pressure of owning. Life was good. I could take vacations, I could travel around the world, and it was beautiful. But then there began to be this pull. I knew that a moment required more.

It's like that moment that you get to the mountaintop and you have to choose to reach back. And you're never on the mountaintop just to absorb the light. You're on the mountaintop to turn into a flashlight to show other people the way. I knew I couldn't just sit on the mountaintop and absorb the light. I knew it was time to turn into a flashlight and to show other people the way. That was ownership for me. I couldn't show people the way as an employee. So I took that leap of faith, and I think it was just timing with my partners and myself. That was just divine timing. I'm grateful for that. I'm grateful to have partners who shared a vision and could share in the weight of the vision.

Kendra: I always say I have the mindset of an intrapreneur and entrepreneur because my goal when I was, like, in sixth grade was to have a career in public relations. And then I was like, I'm going to be the youngest VP at my company. And I did that, and I didn't realize that at the time I was an intrapreneur becoming an entrepreneur. And you think about this notion of divine timing. We have to have a heart for God and be secure in our faith to know that when things happen, it's divine timing.

Angela: And the goal that we keep talking about is when you're living in purpose and you're spiritually led so that when that timing comes, you're ready for it and you know that it's time to receive it. When that divine timing is placed upon us, then we know that it's time. And that trigger might earn the right to be an owner.

Like Angela, having a heart for God has been paramount in my journey of who I am and what I believe to be true about the outcomes of my life.

For me, when I get too far away from my own purpose and heart toward God, I lose focus, I drift, and I am plagued with anxiety. This heart focus comes in many forms from yoga, meditation, prayer, and just being still. I know that work fuels me and powers me, but I also know that work is not my god. My purpose and heart for God is the backbone of what I believe and enables me to show up and keep going daily.

Reclaiming My Own Purpose

Building DBA and navigating my exit was an educational experience to truly own what I'm good at. There was a moment when the people involved had too much control over my personal narrative and vision for myself. Reclaiming my own purpose and passion was myriad in fear and began to be a daily struggle to protect. On every journey, we must take something from it that improves our next experience or teaches us something about ourselves that we have to lean into for future protection and success. Some situations will hurt, some will be the best experiences of your life, and some will change the way you view and live in the world. The beauty is getting to the other side. Your tenacity will keep you going, but you should make sure to tap into and leverage your brain trust community of mentors to educate you on new paths and find financial pathways that reward your value.

Remember: *Sometimes God gives you a "no" or "not yet" to protect you from dangers seen or unseen.*

What side are you on now?

_____

_____

_____

_____

_____

Where are you trying to go?

_____

_____

_____

_____

_____

What is your heart voice saying when you take a moment to breathe?

_____

_____

_____

_____

_____

Find your own purpose and heart for God and take the key pieces you need to navigate to the other side.

Being intentional, being purpose-driven, understanding the responsibility, understanding the call, and doing right by it all.

—Angela Manuel Davis

You Meet Who You Are Supposed to Meet in Divine Time

On June 24, 2022, I moderated two panels during FounderMade, a hybrid live and virtual event that brings together 2,000+ disruptive industry leaders for a day of unparalleled networking opportunities, innovative product and solution discovery, and world-class education. It was in New York, and I had my mom and daughter in tow! My daughter was the ultimate hype girl, sitting front and center and recording the entire panel. After a long day of presenting and talking, we were in the green room preparing to leave, and I heard someone ask if I was Kendra Bracken-Ferguson. The woman standing in front of me was a bundle of energy, a pure light, and as I later learned had a matching heart for God. We had interacted on social media previously, and she had been hoping to meet me. After a long day of doing jazz hands, speaking in front of rooms, and essentially being on for 12 hours, when you are done, you are done. When I first heard my name, I wanted to find every excuse to say I'm just leaving, so let's connect next week; however, that wasn't God's plan, and once again I was reminded of the importance of divine timing.

For me, divine timing has always shown up to be the best timing. It's not my timing; it's God's timing, and when I stop being so focused on what I had planned for that moment in time and let the unknown enter my life at the right time, right second, right day, then there is always goodness. It's like when you're running late because you can't find your keys and you're upset with yourself because now your whole day is late, but then you realize later that those five minutes actually stopped you from being in an accident as you were rushing to your meeting. This happens to me all the time, and instead of stressing out if a meeting is canceled or I miss an event, I trust in the fact that it is divine timing. After all, you meet who you are supposed to meet in divine time.

This particular meeting was with Youmie Jean Francois. I am so glad I stayed that day to meet Youmie, who was building an innovative travel wellness company and later joined BrainTrust Founders Studio becoming one of our most successful wellness founders. We have been friends, colleagues, and supporters ever since.

Youmie Jean Francois is the founder and CEO of Flex-n-Fly, a travel wellness company that provides stretching, yoga, and relaxation classes to travelers before they board their flights. Youmie is an avid traveler, wellness consultant, and speaker. She has been featured in *Forbes*, *Black Enterprise*, *Travel & Leisure*, and TripAdvisor. She speaks four languages fluently and splits her time between New York and Colombia. You can find her attending stretching classes at Flex-n-Fly in airports around the world while bridging the gap between travel and wellness. Keep up with her on Tiktok @flexnfly, Instagram @fexnflyofficial, and flexnfly.com to see when Flex-n-Fly opens up at your airport.

Youmie joined me in season 2 for my 92nd podcast to share how having a heart for God paved the way for her success and acknowledgment of who she is, ultimately an immigrant from Haiti and a New Yorker.

Business of the Beat Excerpt, in Conversation with Youmie Francois

Season 2, Episode 92, November 13, 2022

edited for print

Kendra Bracken-Ferguson
Podcast Host

Youmie Jean Francois
Founder & CEO of Flex-N-Fly

Kendra: What's your journey? What's your story?

Youmie: I think, like many people, that you grow as you age because life has a way of teaching people, and experiences have a way of humbling you in many different ways. I will say that I've always had really great self-confidence, and I think that came from my spirituality.

I have a relationship with God. I like to pray. My confidence doesn't come from what I do or validation from others. It literally comes from God. And when me and God aren't together, it's a mess. There isn't one thing anyone can say to get me back to who I am, because I go to the source, and I see that human beings and experiences are resources, but God is the source. And so for me, that's where I go for my confidence.

Sometimes people aren't sure why I'm so confident, because it doesn't come from a thing, it comes from a spirit. And so it's really hard to infiltrate that because that spirit is consistent, it is bold, it is new, it is constantly changing, but it is also very stable. I find that my confidence only lacks when I'm not all right with God. That's when my self-confidence is at a low. I truly believe in being fully present with yourself.

I think you need to know who you authentically are, and if you don't know, it is absolutely okay for you to figure it out. Like, you don't have to have the answers to everything, but you need to be okay with figuring out the answers. You need to be okay being still because stillness nurtures discovery. So you have to be okay with just being still and saying, you know what? I actually didn't like the feeling that I had with this person, and I have to now make a different decision of whether or not I want to be in the presence of this person. I have to honor myself in a way where when my spirit tells me this isn't okay, I honor that, because I think many of us betray ourselves without recognizing that. And that, again, is wherein lies the lack of self-confidence.

(continued)

I love my life. You couldn't pay me to be anyone else. That gave me Youmie Jean Francois. And I've been through some things. But those things have not broken me. Those things have not hardened me. I've been through so many things in life that the idea and the possibility of it breaking me, of it hardening my heart, of it making me bitter, was so available that my spirit, who I am authentically, could not surrender to that.

My spirit was like, I'm bigger than this in this moment; my word to God and my word to myself means everything to me. Everything to me. And so I honor it. If anyone ever asked me, like, how do you make decisions? I don't make decisions with my heart. I make decisions with my gut. You have to know yourself. It sounds good in general, right? Like, oh, listen to your heart. It's problematic. But my gut is so sure—that's what I have to choose every single time.

Kendra: I think that when people become hardened because of the world, that's where it's just so sad, and we can't allow that to happen, and it can be really hard to get to the other side of that. When we think about validation from God, I know when I'm out of alignment and I realize "Oh, you haven't prayed today; you haven't meditated today. You're spiraling, and you need to ground yourself in something greater than you in order to find your way back," it's my heart for God that brings me back every time.

When I dig deep and reflect on the words of Angela and Youmie and this particular stop on my journey, I see clearly how this experience enabled me as an entrepreneur to reclaim my own purpose and ownership, survive, and ultimately thrive. I remind myself and you to maintain your heart for God or your own higher being, live in purpose, and create your own design for success.

3

Know When to Pivot to Survive and Thrive

Entrepreneurs are a little bit crazy.

When I say that, I don't mean they are obsessive workaholics; you'll find people like that in any type of job, and it's certainly not unique to entrepreneurs.

What I mean instead is that they have a unique relationship with reality. Entrepreneurship is defined by risk. Founders are risk-takers who put their financial security, their careers, and their reputations on the line in pursuit of something as insubstantial as an idea."

—Anne K. Halsall, co-founder and CPO of
Winnie (republished from *Medium*, October 7, 2017)

For the past 25 years, my husband and best friend, Pleas Ferguson, has always supported me. In my last round of building a new company he said, "You can start and build whatever you want, I will always support you; just don't change our lifestyle." Point. Blank. Period.

Kendra and Pleas Ferguson, New York City, 2001

The Story of How I Became an Intrapreneur

I started my career as an intrapreneur, but at that time, I didn't know that's what I was. I just wanted to be a vice president at the largest PR agency in the world, a dream I had aspired to since I was in the sixth grade when I saw the president of the United States preparing to make a speech. As he was preparing to speak, someone walked up to the podium and handed him a note. I turned to my mom and asked who that was, and she said his press secretary. From that moment on, I knew I wanted to be a publicist.

It was later, through much analysis, executive coaching, growth, and true self-actualization, that I realized it was my Taurus personality striving to control the narrative, the direction, and the outcome of the situation. To this day, the most powerful person in the room will always be the publicist—the true connector, holder of information, and architect of storytelling. My roots and passion will always be in public relations (PR). For me, PR evolved into social media, influencer marketing, and digital marketing—truly all the most modern forms of communication.

According to Wikipedia,

A publicist is a person whose job is to generate and manage publicity for a company, a brand, or public figure—especially a celebrity—or for a work such as a book, film, or album. Publicists are public relations specialists who have the role to maintain and represent the images of individuals, rather than representing an entire corporation or business.

In my experience, sometimes PR professionals get a bad rap as being spin artists, stretchers of truth, or fluffy. What I love about PR is the ability to make perception reality, create stories that influence people, and ultimately steer the directional impact of reputation.

With my goals set on a career as a publicist, I graduated from Round Rock High School in Round Rock, Texas, and went to Purdue University in West Lafayette, Indiana, armed with a scholarship and a declared major to study communications and public relations. I had three core goals in college: to participate in everything, work hard/play hard, and graduate with enough experience, volunteering, and contacts to land my dream job. I was the president of my sorority, Sigma Gamma Rho, I was a Purdue Golduster, I danced for the Jahari Dance Troupe, I was the senior writer for the Black Cultural Center newsletter, and I interned in the athletic department as well as for the Indiana Pacers. I was seen, I was out, and while I loved and still love a good party, I *never* missed class.

At Purdue University, I met Kathryn Jordan, who at the time was one of the only Black women to be at the NBA for over 25 years and was the vice president of team and player development. To this day, I credit Kathy as giving me my first big corporate opportunity to experience the inner workings of business structure and the catalyst to piquing my interest in working with talent. The Indiana Pacers offered me my first internship outside of Purdue University and thrust me into a world of player and community relations. I supported the communications team, handled the family room during game days, and helped with all of our community programming. I was so deeply rooted in sports, as an intern in the Purdue athletics department and later marrying my college sweetheart, who played basketball in college. With Kathy's help, I secured a scholarship to get my master's in sports administration. That is where the plot thickens . . .

Before I was able to pursue my master's, live in Indiana, and work full-time for the Pacers, I was offered a job at FleishmanHillard NY, one of the largest PR agencies in the world. I had spent the prior summer interning in the consumer department.

Part of my plan during college was to get an internship at one of the top five PR agencies in the world. I researched and researched until I found the HR person at each company and applied for their summer internship programs. Brandon Carter and Kristen Bright who I met the first day of college and are still two of my best friends to this day, and I took the Greyhound bus from West Lafayette to New York City to interview for our respective internships. It was my first cross-country trip on a Greyhound bus and my first time in New York. With our college money, we had just enough to stay in a hostel in Times Square. After my first meeting with the team at Fleishman, I was offered an internship the following summer in their New York office.

Brandon Carter (far right), Kristen Bright, Pleas Ferguson, Kendra (front center), Tricey Wilks (far left) in 2000

When summer 2001 rolled around, my boyfriend (and now husband) Pleas, sorority sister Tricey Wilks, Brandon, and I loaded up my mother's Camry and took a road trip from New York to Purdue. The plan was for Pleas and Tricey to drop me and Brandon off at a friend's house in Brooklyn. We had met this friend in New York the previous summer while interviewing for our internships, as neither of us had enough money to pay for housing in New York to work our internships. However, as with all coming-of-age stories, we arrived in New York and couldn't find our "friend" (who we had only met once, by the way, and had kept in touch with by writing letters).

March 2001, New York City, Times Square: Kendra (far left), Kristen Bright, Brandon Carter, and unknown pen pal (far right)

We were left with jobs starting on Monday, nowhere to live, and a bank account lacking multiple zeros to pay our own way. As any resilient 20-year-old who did not want to go back to West Lafayette for another summer would do, we pivoted. We called Brandon's frat brother, the only person we knew in New York, cried, and shared our story of being "homeless" in New York. He immediately gave us a solution: come live with him, his mother, and his grandmother for the summer in Far Rockaway, Queens. And just like that, we moved in with his family, the last stop on the A Train in Queens, and spent the summer commuting almost four hours each way to fulfill our destiny, all while sharing a room with our friend's grandmother.

That experience was tough, and it was scary at times, but it was an amazing pivot on my journey. I grew up about 10 years that summer and was even more laser-focused on reaching my career goals.

At that point, I was about to graduate and had set my mind on moving to Indianapolis with Pleas, working at the Pacers, and getting my master's—until I got a call from FleishmanHillard, offering me a role as an assistant account executive. The only catch was that I had to be in their New York office in two weeks to start working on my first client, Mary Kay Cosmetics. I immediately accepted the offer and started down the path that would later turn into my first stint as an intrapreneur.

Now, moving to New York in two weeks is no small feat, and for someone with no family or real friends in New York, a bank account still lacking zeros and really nowhere to go, I had to act fast. The first order of business was to figure out housing.

This was 2002, and without that bank account or an old rich aunt, my options were extremely limited. What I did find was nun's housing that was run by the Catholic church for professional women just moving to New York who were in need of housing. All I needed was a letter from my job and a commitment to keep my room clean and be in the house in my room by 10 p.m. every night. Shortly after that, I secured my first apartment and my family and now-husband loaded up the U-Haul and drove cross-country to officially move me and my furniture to New York.

Through both of my spontaneous moves to New York, my ability to pivot ultimately led me to experiences that forever changed the trajectory of my career. I would have simply missed the moment. From this I learned:

- Roll with the punches. Be unstoppable in your pursuit to fulfill your dreams and pivot when you hit dead ends and wrong turns.
- Exhaust every option before you determine there is no way to make it happen.
- Don't let money or the lack thereof keep you from experiences that could forever change your life; be honest about what you need.
- Trust your brain trust; neither Brandon nor I had ever been to Far Rockaway, Queens, but we made it through that summer together. From Kristen, Brandon, and I taking the Greyhound bus to New York, to Pleas and Tricey driving us to New York, to Brandon's frat brother's family welcoming us into their home, to our unshakable trust in each other, it is that trust that we still have to this day.

Take a moment and think about an unplanned pivot you had to make in the early days of your career. What are three to five positive outcomes that came because you were willing to pivot?

_____

_____

_____

_____

_____

In 2002, I started my first professional full-time job at FleishmanHillard New York. I was an assistant account executive, trying to rise through the ranks and secure my first promotion, taking on as much as I could to be seen and promoted. My boss, Heidi Hoveland, who at the time was senior vice president and senior partner/director, was an inspiration and was one of the best examples of a leader I have had throughout my entire career. She was charming, smart, open to ideas, and fully supportive of everyone in the team. She dazzled the room in new business presentations and gave clear feedback for improvements. To this day, she is someone I can call and ask for advice or just talk shop.

I was also fortunate enough to have a parallel reporting structure to Alan Rambam, who during this time was the senior vice president and senior partner of Mobile, Social, and Youth. More than anything, he is a visionary and an innovator, way ahead of his time, and one of the best people in business I have ever met. Together Alan and I stayed up all night and wrote what we believed was the manifesto for how FleishmanHillard would take on digital PR, later known as *social media*. This was back in 2004, so our vernacular of social media wasn't as astute and defined as it is today, but we had a vision and plan to pivot into this new area of Web 2.0.

Alan, being Alan, got our ideas passed by top leadership, including the CEO, and off we went . . . to London, to Hong Kong, to Beijing, to Korea, and all over Canada, preaching to whoever would listen about social media and this new thing called social networks. At the time we worked with the founders at Community Connect, who had started Black Planet, Mi Gente, and Asian Avenue. My job consisted of being on message boards and forums all day, and we launched the first social media, user, and brand partnership between MySpace and Cingular Wireless to create the Mobile Music Studio.

We went on to work on the first campaigns on Facebook when it was just launched and was an .edu. We saw the opportunity and seized the day. Over the course of seven years, we helped build the digital practice group at Fleishman, launched the mobile and youth practice, and helped shepherd in this new form of "digital PR." Looking back, I wasn't just an assistant account executive trying to be a boss; I was starting my journey as an intrapreneur.

Moving on Up

After many years at Fleishman, I got the bug to go in-house and was recruited by Ralph Lauren to be their first director of digital media. My roots will always be tied to the agency world, but I wanted to experience something new and different. I am a firm believer that working for an agency early in your career gives you a different type of muscle around flexibility, pivots, and customer service. You are serving the needs of your clients and generally you have three to six clients at one time who all need your attention, care, and brain to run their accounts.

Fleishman was unique because it was so large; I was able to work across multiple offices, with different teams, and while my focus was always consumer packaged goods, particularly fashion and beauty, the breadth of my work was cross-industry and global.

Going to Ralph Lauren was a dream come true. After being in the agency life for so long, I was excited to focus on one brand. I also really liked the idea of a "team" mentality; having cheered and danced through high school and college and being part of a sorority, there is something about wearing the same uniform, aligning on the collective win, and having a group of people marching toward the same goal and focus.

As the first director of digital media, the scope of my job was broad and multifaceted with many bosses and directions; however, my day-to-day was led by Julie Berman, who at the time was the senior vice president of corporate communications. Julie and I are still close. She continues to be a champion, ally, and friend, and I can count on her to show up.

When I went to Ralph Lauren, the job was seemingly perfect. I worked for a family-led global fashion brand and was leading the charge on social media. I launched the brand across Facebook and Twitter (Instagram didn't exist yet) and got to go to the Olympics posting photos of the athletes wearing Ralph Lauren. I spent hours sitting with the ultimate intrapreneur and head of marketing, David Lauren, looking at new ways to work with bloggers under his idea of Merchantainment. I also worked with the CFO to show just how much money we were generating from this new thing called social media marketing and creating global initiatives centered around social media and bloggers. Although on paper I was part of the corporate communications team, I was truly a team of one with my expertise and focus. Looking back I wasn't just the first director of digital media, I was an intrapreneur, building within the confines of a larger institutional structure.

> "We have to get to a place where we celebrate the evolutions of business within our community. The beauty of being an entrepreneur is your ability to pivot."
> —Lisa Price, founder of Carol's Daughter

The Story of How I Became an Entrepreneur

During my time at Ralph Lauren, two pivotal things happened that shaped my perspective and solidified my future as an entrepreneur.

The first was that I had the extreme fortune to join a meeting with Ralph Lauren and his wealth management team. At the time, Mr. Lauren was focused on buying back some of his licenses, a decision he said he made early in the days of building Ralph Lauren when the company needed capital and support to scale. That meeting planted a seed in me to want one day my own wealth management team gathered around a boardroom table talking about the future of my own company and strategizing for extreme growth and success. Mr. Lauren came to work every day, he participated, and he inspired me beyond measure as the first successful self-made entrepreneur I had ever met.

The second instrumental moment was meeting Karen Robinovitz, who would later be my co-founder at Digital Brand Architects. I met Karen only once in person and spoke to her a few times on the phone before we decided to start the company together.

One Friday night several months after meeting her I couldn't get her out of my head, so I woke up Saturday morning and texted her. She called me back within 30 minutes, a quality that I came to love. (I always try to emulate Karen and respond to emails, calls, and texts promptly, to this day.) I told her I had an idea to manage bloggers as talent, and she said, "Me too!"

We wasted no time getting started. She already had a company name ready to go—Digital Brand Architects—that she had been trying to determine how to use, so that same day we published a temporary website, and the next day, we got our husbands together for brunch so they could meet. On Monday we filed for an LLC, and I went to David Lauren and told him I was going to manage bloggers. He said that as long as they were wearing Ralph Lauren, everything was all good. And just like that we started Digital Brand Architects with a vision and a greenfield of opportunity.

To us, it was clear that bloggers were going to be the next big thing and the future of the digital space. Our earliest clients— Aimee Song, Something Navy, Bagsnob—were bloggers who turned into eight-figure brand owners, leaders, and some of the

---

most influential innovators of our time. Looking back, this experience forever changed my internal wiring and psychology around business ownership. I became an entrepreneur.

After finding success as an entrepreneur at DBA and then ultimately deciding to leave, I spent time examining the role I played in the demise of the relationship with my business partners and reflecting on what I learned. I instituted weekly "homework" to seek guidance through writing to reflect, recognize, and reorganize myself and my direction forward. This is a practice that I learned through my dear friend and longtime executive coach, Julie Flanders. Writing your thoughts regularly is a cleansing practice; it helps you to articulate your dreams, pain points, challenges, and desired success without judgment or dancing around other people's feelings. It is just for you. I look back on my writings often to see if there are patterns I am falling back into, if there are lessons to be learned, and to see all that I have accomplished. It becomes a tool for manifesting and creating new pathways to actualize your goals.

Every year, Julie shares a few prompts to set the stage to welcome in a new year of possibilities and encourages her clients to adapt and write their own. My prompts are ever-changing, based on my year. Here is a sample of where I landed in 2023:

- What are three to five big audacious goals for next year?
- What did you learn this year?
- How will what you learned guide your decisions for next year?
- What caused you pain this year? How did you resolve it?

- What caused you joy this year? Why was it joyful?
- Did you maintain your core brain trust? Who did you lose and why?
- What do you regret that you didn't do? How are you going to leave that regret in this year and not carry it into a new year of magic?
- Where was your faith challenged? How did you restore your faith?
- What tools do you already possess to reach your goals?
- What do you want to learn next year?
- What is your word for your next year? Why this word? What does it mean in the dictionary? What does it mean to you?
- What pivots do you need to make to accomplish your goals?
- What are prompts you want to explore?

_____

_____

_____

_____

_____

We are all magical and have the power to manifest our destinies through true self-actualization. My clarity comes from my weekly "homework," prayer, meditation, and my belief that God would not bring me on this journey to stay in a valley of doubt but for me to rise to mountains of abundance. For me, self-actualization is unlocked through writing and finding those moments to clarify the pivots needed to continue on the journey. The truth found through writing unlocks vision, feelings, wishes, wants, and desires. When we can write and articulate freely, we are igniting the path for the magic and greatness to happen. We have to work hard, be kind, and push forward.

> "Some you win and some you lose. Be glad when you win. Don't have regrets when you lose."
>
> —Richard Branson

Through self-actualization, putting my key learnings to work, seeing my purpose, and resetting my mind, I did what I knew how to do: I embraced my destiny as an entrepreneur and started my own company, BrainTrust.

Why the name *BrainTrust*? Throughout my career I have relished being part of a team. I remember writing in my journal a year prior about a few key learnings from my past experiences that did not turn out as I had hoped. The underlying theme that came up time and time again in my journal entries was trying to do it myself, not asking for help, and trying to execute outside of my best talents and strengths in a silo. Two words kept radiating in my head and I wrote the words on a whiteboard in my office:

- BRAIN: I love smart people, I love smart conversations, I love thinkers, and I love brainstorms.
- TRUST: What I underestimated when I was building my first company is that trust is the core of everything. Just because you share a really good idea with someone does not mean you have mutual integrity and trust. It's important to trust who you are working with every day. As you build your brain trust, instill trust from the beginning and

claim it as a core value. The blessing of having "trust part-ners," not just business partners, is the ability to create posi-tivity through the shared alignment of caring about each other's well-being, your team, and the outcomes that max-imize the greater good for all.

It was that realization that I decided to name my company BrainTrust (all one word) symbolizing that in business the two must go hand in hand.

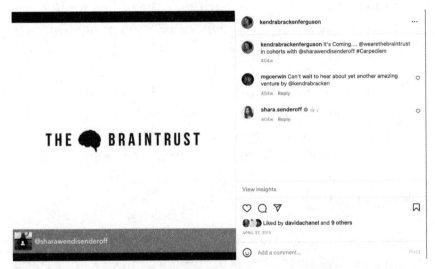

First post on Instagram, April 27, 2015, of initial BrainTrust logo created by Shara Senderoff

BrainTrust was and continues to be very personal for me. Both the name and our work was a culmination of what I learned from my past experiences. BrainTrust is the manifesta-tion of my first pillar of **community**: a group of brains coming together to solve problems, formulate an idea, or make some-thing happen. We weren't meant to work in silos or be on our own creating and driving innovation. I also want to be in a trusting community with people that I trust to do what they say, be kind, and ready for whatever turn-up we need to make it happen.

When I started BrainTrust, it was meant to be a consultancy of smart business executives coming together to solve problems. My vision was the ultimate whiteboarding session of not only problems but solutions that we would publish together. What BrainTrust became is a global brand marketing firm working with some of the biggest celebrities, brands, and institutions. And in the process I was an entrepreneur again, running a digital agency.

The path to entrepreneurship is different for everyone. Sometimes you start there; sometimes you evolve into it after experiencing life as an intrapreneur. Regardless, the path of entrepreneurship comes with great sacrifice, commitment, and a belief outside of yourself that you will be successful no matter what, no matter when.

It wasn't until she was in her 50s that Angel Cornelius became an entrepreneur. She is the founder and CEO of Maison 276, a sophisticated collection of luxurious beauty products created with plant-based, sustainable ingredients that Angel created and formulated in her kitchen that has grown into a nationally recognized and distributed beauty brand. For more than two years, while building her own business, she worked as an intrapreneur, leading clinics and developing programs during the day and creating formulas and launching products at night. When we talk about sacrifices that lead to entrepreneurship, Angela proved that those sacrifices lead to big rewards no matter your age or stage in life.

Business of the Beat **Excerpt, in Conversation with Angel Cornelius**

Season 2, Episode 3, February 13, 2022

edited for print

Kendra Bracken-Ferguson
Business of the Beat Host

Angel Cornelius
CEO & Founder
Maison 276

Angel: I just kept making products and experimenting, and I had this little black book that I call "my book of failures" because I took very copious notes of what worked and what didn't, and I came up with stuff that worked for me, and I was perfectly happy.

(*continued*)

And that is, as my son likes to say, when I became a real business. It was just like one of the hardest things I've ever had to do at that point. There were many days I sat in my office at Texas Children's Hospital, and that was one of the clinics that I ran and just thought, What in the world did I get myself into? But that is how it started, just purely organic and just literally learning on the run. Just learning. I heard someone say at the time that being an entrepreneur is like jumping out of a plane and building a parachute on the way down. I was not going to be that person who didn't come through.

Whatever it took, we were going to figure this out, and I was going to deliver what I said I was going to deliver. And it started this incredible, amazing journey. As a 50+ entrepreneur who never even thought of doing anything like that, it's just been amazing.

Kendra: At what point, did you say, I'm going to leave the clinic and do this full time? Because in 2016, it sounds like you were still running the clinic and building the brand?

Angel: I was staying up until 2 a.m. in the morning, doing whatever needed to be done, getting about four or five hours of sleep, going to work, and then doing it all over again. I mean, I would go to the post office on my lunch to mail orders to my customers. Building the company was integrated into every part of my life. And I told myself, when my daytime job inhibits the growth of the business, that's when I know it's time for me to take a leap of faith. And I was very methodical. I didn't wake up one morning and say, okay, I'm giving them two weeks' notice. I decided in January of 2017 that was going to be my last year at the clinic.

So I had a whole year of doing whatever lifestyle adjustments I needed to do. Emotionally preparing, financially preparing. We're a bootstrapped, self-funded company. When I walked out of that clinic in December 2017, I didn't know what was ahead, but I knew I had to do this or I would never forgive myself.

Every entrepreneur comes to that decision in a different way at a different time. And there's no one size fits all. You have to do it at the time that you think is right for you. And I will tell you, in January of 2018, literally two weeks from when I had retired, opportunities came to me that I would not have been able to take advantage of if I was still employed. A full-time accelerator program through the Columbia School of Business in New York and all of these opportunities came within weeks of retiring. And so I knew that was a confirmation. This is the time, and this is what it means to happen.

Kendra: In two weeks, all these opportunities started to fall into place. I think it's faith, preparedness, and readiness that takes us on this journey. And being able to share that, because so many people say, I'm in this job, I'm scared for the leap. What do I do? And you were truly one of the first people who has taken a year to say, let me do this right, and let me prepare myself. Because it's not just my two weeks' notice; it's the mental shift that has to happen to move into something new as an entrepreneur.

Angel: I will be honest with you, it's scary. I could have retired in five years. So I decided to start all over again in an industry that I had no experience in beyond what I had created here in my home. And that's why I say becoming an

(continued)

entrepreneur and starting your own business is such a personal decision because you do have to be at peace and understand that you don't know exactly what's going to be ahead. But let me just tell you, it's going to be hard. And if you don't want hard, then this might not be for you. And maybe this isn't the time.

Kendra: It's the high highs and the low lows. I think that's what makes the entrepreneurial spirit a gift and a curse.

Angel: It's all these parts of me that I think prepared me for this at this stage in life. I just have so many life experiences that I didn't think about until in retrospect. And so one of the things that I do say to women who are considering pivoting to anything at this stage, don't undervalue the value of your lifetime experience. You have expertise in so many areas that you are not even aware of because you just live it every day. It's decades of work. Don't discount that just because you want to drive in a new lane. You bring all of that with you.

And I feel like I brought all of that with me. And even in my jobs, I always viewed every position as an entrepreneur, because if that was my department to run, it was mine to run and succeed in. It was mine to grow and to build a team. So in retrospect, I definitely feel like I've always had an entrepreneur's mindset. This is just the first time I've actually had the label of entrepreneur.

For me, like Angel, the true testament to my career as an entrepreneur are the steps and experiences that I had along the way. Each step builds on top of the others to pave a way for me to embrace, accept, and learn from my wins, losses, lessons. When I think about each career move I've made and the brain trust of supporters and champions who have helped me recognize my gifts and my value in whatever role I play, these are the true gifts that I will take with me from experience to experience. Each day is a new day to start again, to pursue a dream, to reconcile a relationship, or to take a new path to jumpstart the next journey.

So how do you label your career?

_____

_____

_____

_____

_____

What value do you place on your lifetime of experiences that are steps along your journey?

_____

_____

_____

_____

_____

"I woke up. I looked up. I praise You, God, for a brand-new day, and the blessings of a new week. I have a roof over my head. My daily bread. Running water. Clothes to wear. My family is healthy. I'm not lucky, Lord. I'm Blessed!"

4 | Ego: Who, Me?

Ego is important. Without a healthy ego entrepreneurs don't have the necessary internal reserves to survive the daily rigors of startup life.

—Ben Yoskovitz, *Instigator* blog, July 22, 2010

I never thought I had an ego until I became an intrapreneur for the third time and my ego reared its ugly little head in a way that I had never experienced. This time around, going back into someone else's company as an intrapreneur was different; my mindset was forever altered as I had just spent the years prior as an entrepreneur. I had already successfully started and run two companies and had been a working entrepreneur for about eight years, managing my team, making decisions, and running the show. My ego wasn't driven by having to compete with entitled peers, politics, or an industry that praises and rewards employee competition. Instead, my ego was driven by a need to keep my company afloat, make payroll, and pay office rent.

When your ego becomes entwined in a political chess game, a true entrepreneur who is playing the role of intrapreneur (as I was during this stop on my journey) simply cannot win. As an

67

entrepreneur, my focus was solely on getting it done and moving forward as the sole provider for my team and captain of our ship. Going back into corporate life as an intrapreneur at that point was difficult, and, I admit, my ego got the best of me trying to defend myself, my talents, and my own vision against the backdrop of interoffice politics and bad corporate behavior.

What I learned through this transition is that ego can become a detractor rather than a tool to help accomplish your goals when you are not in the right environment that rewards your natural gifts and talents. A healthy ego is defined through the lens of meekness and self-actualization. We all need an ego, whether we are intrapreneurs or entrepreneurs, because a healthy ego will protect you, help ensure that you are treated fairly, and help others value your uniqueness. After all, no one has the same DNA as you, and we are individually brilliant in our own talents, which should be celebrated and applauded.

What Is Ego?

Everyone has an ego. There are many definitions of the ego, but to put it simply, it's your sense of personal identity or feelings of self-importance. It helps you to identify your "uniqueness," to stand up for yourself and to put plans into action.

It is, however, incredibly important that you notice how your ego impacts your decisions as it can be a negative influence. If you can think of a time when you've done or said something that had negative consequences, this was your misguided ego at play.

Having an awareness of your ego plays a large part in improving your relationships with others, as well as your ability to manage others and yourself. I have found that becoming more aware of my ego has made me happier.

Excerpt from "How Your Ego Is Affecting Your Mental Health" by Alex Morris, www.ihasco.co.uk/blog/entry/2206/ get-to-know-your-ego, posted 2019.

A Valuable Lesson Around the Self-Serving Sabotage of Ego

I learned another valuable lesson about ego in business in May 2020, during a super-rough trip to New York. It was by far one of the most mentally challenging business trips I had experienced in a long time. We were just coming out of beta for BrainTrust Founders Studio and starting to fundraise for BrainTrust Fund. While I generally travel to New York every month or two for work, I am generally solo and navigate the city, my schedule, my time, and my meetings as I see fit.

This time was different, as I was traveling with several new people in the company and was being pulled from meeting to event, on someone else's schedule that was not my own. In hindsight, I could have reset the calendar and talked more productively and openly with my colleagues about the goals of the trip, but at the end of the day, it lent itself to activating my pillar of **education**. Ego shows up in funny ways—ways that can catch you off guard and force you to check yourself. During this moment, I found myself reflecting on how ego manifests and changes with age, circumstance, and the power I hold in various situations.

Ultimately, that week in New York I lost balance because I allowed my ego to get in the way of asking for and receiving help. In this instance, I was running around the city in back-to-back meetings and juggling my team's needs alongside simply not having the brain space to get my own work done, causing sensory overload. Now, there will always be overly busy moments in business, and when they happen, it is imperative to reassess the situation and determine where help is needed, what can be delegated, and how to maintain your center. As the leader, you must set the example of activating your team efficiently so everyone participates and has ownership in completing all that needs to be done.

The moment of self-actualization that I was being my own worst enemy came via a simple text message at the end of a particularly hard meeting, where I should have been asking for help but instead approached the meeting with ego telling me I was the only one who could save the day. As a result, in the meeting I was deeply guarded and standoffish, which was out of character for me. I was in utter despair, contemplating how I was going to get everything done that I had decided to take on myself. It was at that moment I opened my phone and this message appeared in the form of a Bible verse:

> Today's Prayer: Father, I pray that I will ask for help when I need it, receive support when someone offers it, and never walk in pride or independence when You send help to me.
>
> 1 Samuel 25:23–44

Wow, smack in my face! I realized I needed to reset and stop using my ego to block the blessing of help. As entrepreneurs, we wear this cape that says "I've got this," but asking for help is the most courageous thing we can do.

In reality, we can't do everything alone, and often, especially as women, moms, friends, and wives, we want to support everyone and do everything without asking for assistance or "bothering" those around us. Do any of the following statements sound familiar to you?

- "I'll just do it."
- "They are too busy to help."
- "I'll just handle it—I know what's best."
- "It's my job to do it and so let me put my head down and solve it."

That's where my ego got the best of me; it stopped me from receiving the help I needed to actualize my vision in the form of service to my community.

Your Ego's Job Is to Feel Important

When I paused and meditated on the verse and my behavior, I found that my center was off because I was allowing my ego to push me into not asking and therefore not receiving. Self-inflicted mental strife, significant time lost, discomfort in my relationships . . . all because I was overcome by ego.

To quote Alex Morris again:

Your ego's job is to feel important. Its survival depends on it. Unfortunately, this translates to your ego needing to fight and defend itself. It seems counterintuitive, but the ego needs negative situations to arise so it can have something to do, something to worry about, or something to change. So if you're happy, and everything is perfect, your ego will already be looking for an issue to cling to or a drama to create.. . . The problems arise when it affects your decision making, your mood, or it turns you into a victim, an underdog, or it makes you feel superior to others in order to justify your behavior. These things make you miserable. Your ego will fight this fact though, it wants to look at the past and the future to find trouble so it can defend itself. It wants to fight. It doesn't want you to be at peace. Your ego needs an enemy—a situation or a problem to feel bigger or better than. This stops you from enjoying your life and accepting things as they are. You can, however, learn to accept how things are by simply noticing when your ego is interfering and gently bringing it back into line.

Through self-actualization, I was able to bring myself back in line, reconnect to my greater *why*, and talk out what was driving this part of my ego to appear. Once I reset, slept, meditated, and went to a place of gratefulness, I felt re-anchored, balanced, and centered.

What I know for certain is that this won't be the last time ego creeps in to disrupt the help needed to advance the good. Allowing grace and faith to balance my ego enables me to acknowledge, receive, and move into open space where I consciously and intentionally accept help from others. To give is to receive.

Understanding Your Own Ego

As we dive into ego, I invite you to think about your own. How can you stay open to receiving help that moves your vision forward without allowing the voice of ego to whisper to keep you from asking what you need?

_____

_____

_____

_____

_____

I've kept an email since 2019 from Isis Arias, a creative marketer, coach, writer, and friend, who created a newsletter called *Pep Talk Tuesdays,* and this is one for the books—in fact *it's the best of all time!*

Excerpt from Isis Arias newsletter, *Pep Talk Tuesdays*

Tuesday, April 9, 2019

edited for print

PEP TALK TUESDAYS

Humility is important. Being humble is a wonderful trait; hubris and arrogance never were items that someone wished for, but sometimes you gotta get in there and F*CK SH*T UP.

Sometimes you gotta remind 'em. And sometimes you gotta remind YOURSELF!

Say it with me:

I'M THE BEST TO EVER DO IT.

I GOT MYSELF HERE AND I'M GONNA KEEP ON GOING.

NO ONE IS GOING TO HOLD ME BACK AND ESPECIALLY NOT MYSELF.

IF I NEED TO GET IT, I'M GON' GET IT!

This may be in reference to those haters DJ Khaled told y'all about, or it may just be those internal creeping doubts that keep telling you you're not good enough. Who told you you were less than? And why the hell did you believe em??

Remember—Kanye told you he was the best rapper in the world when he was still in a pink polo and rocking a

(continued)

backpack selling beats. (Feel how you feel about him now, but the man's a household name regardless.)

Barry Bonds, said "I'm not arrogant, I'm good—there's a difference."

Jay said, "I'm not a businessman; I'M A BUSINESS, MAN." And look at all the businesses he done built.

Muhammad Ali talked ALL the sh*t! It was partially a tactic for his opponents and made for great TV, but he also kept the mindstate of being the best.

PS—I'm often about leaving an ego at the door—but sometimes you have to stroke your own if it means that it will push you further or get you through.

The Intersection of Meekness and Ego

As I've said, all entrepreneurs have an ego. Well, from my experience, all intrapreneurs have an ego too . . . and all egos must be tempered by humility. God will humble you before He exalts you. Being an intrapreneur was humbling for me.

Entrepreneurs live by their ego—a no-nonsense mentality that you *can* and you *will* be successful. I mean, the thought of not being successful never crossed my mind.

"We all fall in love with our own ideas."
—George Kaiser (November 3, 2022), as shared first-hand by Mr. Kaiser in a meeting we were in together)

It struck me at church one day as I was listening to a message by Faithful Central Bishop Kenneth C. Ulmer that one of the hardest jobs is being a minister, a preacher, a bishop—you will always be an intrapreneur living the life of an entrepreneur. Depending on what you believe, your boss is a spiritual being, and you will never have His job or create what He designed.

This realization shifted my intention to look through the spiritual lens of ego and reminded me of a conversation I had with my longtime eyelash artist, Tussanee Luebbers about the notion of meekness and ego.

She summarized the intersection between the two, proclaiming, "Meekness is cloaking your strength and tempering your ego so you can use it for a greater good later."

And in one of Bishop Ulmer's sermons from June 13, 2014, he says, *"Meek Not Weak, But Happy."*

Kendra and Tussanee Luebbers, Lash Artist, Speaker, Consultant, Podcast Co-Host of LashCast, & Co-Founder of the largest lash conference in the world: The LASHCONference backstage at LashCon November 2022.

What if we acknowledge that a needed characteristic for developing a healthy ego is meekness? Not as a meek person but under the guise of spiritual meekness, it's not about ego; it's about healthy self-worth.

> Being meek does not mean weakness, but it does mean behaving with goodness and kindness, showing strength, serenity, healthy self-worth, and self-control. Meekness was one of the most abundant attributes in the Savior's life. He Himself taught His disciples, "Learn of me; for I am meek and lowly in heart."
> —Elder Ulisses Soares of the Presidency of the Seventy

As we translate the notion of meekness into leadership both through the lens of intrapreneurship and entrepreneurship, it seems that meek leaders are effective leaders because they are humble. It takes humility to listen, humility to collaborate, and humility to show up in service to your team. It ultimately takes a humble ego to disagree without being disagreeable.

When we think about meekness as a characteristic of ego, there are few considerations:

Know your truth and express self-confidence in all that you do. The theologian A. W. Tower spoke extensively on meekness, writing, "The meek man cares not at all who is greater than he, for he has long ago decided that the esteem of the world is not worth the effort." At the end of the day, we must lean into the confidence mindset reflected in our ego. Be confident in our talents. Being a leader can be lonely; you may not always win the popularity contest, but know your truth and be steadfast in what you bring to the table.

On a scale of 1 to 5, how much emphasis do you place on being liked by all and applauded for every decision you make?

Why does it matter? Or does it?

_____

_____

_____

_____

_____

Meekness has been described as power under control. Brandon Cox wrote about meekness in an October 3, 2014, blog post entitled "Meekness Is the Leverage of Leadership," and he referred to how the word was used in the Bible. He wrote,

> The Bible's word for meekness is used in reference to a broken horse, which has all the power to destroy its rider but refrains out of respect for authority. The word is also used to refer to a soldier who has all the might to take on the enemy, yet submits himself completely to the authority of his commanding officer. Meekness is the key to having leverage in leadership. It's the refusal to demand respect in exchange for commanding it with a life of integrity. It is "controlled power." Meekness is the willingness to suppress those urges to lash out at the wrong time, opting instead to wait for further orders from our commanding officer, Jesus.

Throughout my career, when I have reacted in haste, the outcomes have not been as favorable for me. Meekness is practicing the notion of self-control that we abstain from functioning in a reactive state based on the behavior of others but we are, rather, guided, thoughtful, and measured in our responses.

Describe a time where your self-control was absent and the outcome was not favorable?

_____

_____

_____

_____

_____

Describe a time where your self-control was present and the outcome was favorable?

_____

_____

_____

_____

_____

Understand what is important and necessary to actualize your vision within the pillars you have determined to be guiding principles in business. At the end of the day, that is all that matters. Protect your time, energy, and mind against those things that at the end of the day are not important to reaching your goals. They are trivial nuisances that are meant to throw us off our guard and slow us down.

Ken Gosnell writes in his post "The Secret Leadership Traits—MEEKNESS" (November 24, 2015):

Meek leaders don't fight every leadership battle. They are self-directed to determine the battles that need their time and energy. They are not afraid to fight, but they don't waste their time that is not important to their overall vision. Meek leaders know how to let things go. They hold things loosely. They leave yesterday behind them so that they can focus all of their energy and effort on the task that they face at the moment.

Across my pillars—community, mentorship, education, and capital—I will always fight for what is right and important.

- **Community:** I will fight to build a community rooted in being of service to each other, showing kindness, and being respectful and giving.
- **Mentorship:** I will fight to ensure that mentorship is at the center of growth and development for me and my team.
- **Education:** I will fight to ensure that we have access to knowledge, tools, and the resources we need to successfully grow our businesses.
- **Capital:** I will fight to ensure that there is representation in venture and that capital is distributed to underrepresented communities.

What is worth fighting for to you?

_____

_____

_____

_____

_____

One final thought about meekness from A. W. Tower: "The meek man is not a human mouse afflicted with a sense of his own inferiority. Rather he may be in his moral life as bold as a lion and as strong as Samson; but he has stopped being fooled about himself. Yes, the world needs more meek leaders. Leaders that don't think they have it all figured out. Leaders who know themselves and their weaknesses and are strong enough to be authentic and still lead with boldness and determination."

The Role of Self-Actualization When Confronting Your Ego

For me self-actualization is another important characteristic when it comes to ego that entrepreneurs should consider cultivating. It rules all areas of business growth as a leader.

The year 2022 was one of growth for me. I removed people and things, and gained courage and raised my expectations of how people should show up for me based on how I show up for them. I also realized through deep conversations with one of my close friends and business associates, Farrah Louviere Cerf, that sometimes people show up the best they can, and that's all we can expect from them. She taught me to not just listen when people worry about my health or time but to, more importantly, think about *"How I value my YESes."* Every ounce of energy we give is an ounce of energy that we can't give to something else. I choose to understand my value and prioritize my time.

"I Said Yes to Everything"

Continuing this discussion of time, I'm drawn to a conversation I had with Dionne Phillips, founder of D'Lashes, in season 1 of my podcast. Dionne said, "Time is my business, so I have to make sure that I'm on point with that."

Dionne shared her candid experience as a model, product innovator, and luxury lash spa owner. She shared her fascination with fashion and modeling as a girl growing up in Ohio and the opportunities that guided her to New York City at 19. One day as she did her makeup on set, she cut a pair of lashes and added them to the edge of her own; this bold move created an enhanced, natural-looking, "extended wear" lash trend that would later become her signature. This look resonated early on with celebrities including Brandy, Serena Williams, and so many more who tweeted about getting their lashes done in Dionne's kitchen.

As Dionne modeled around the world and offered her lash service, her passion changed. Her observation, study, and experimentation led to her becoming a respected licensed professional and pioneer of trends in the lash industry. As a successful lash artist for more than 20 years, she has also developed several innovative technologies, including 3D lashes.

Dionne talks about transitioning from formulas to manufacturing to product development. She offers a diverse portfolio of products and services beyond lashes. She goes deep into the close relationships that she forms with her clients through her work, from trust-building dialogue, and 1:1 consulting, where she helped them apply their own lashes during COVID. Lastly, she shares the catalysts for her tenacity as a wife, mother, mentor, and educator. Upon writing this, Dionne was diagnosed with breast cancer and has reflected on being away from her work, the importance of family, and the balance she has found during this phase.

Business of the Beat Excerpt, in Conversation with Dionne Phillips, Founder, D'Lashes

Season 1, Episode 46: October 24, 2021

edited for print

WITH DIONNE PHILLIPS
HOSTED BY KENDRA BRACKEN-FERGUSON

Dionne: I grew up as this young, actually shy girl, very observant of other people, and I grew up in pageants. I was a pageant girl. I wanted to be Miss Ohio, Miss America. That was my thing. From that I transitioned into modeling. Of course, inspired by my mom, she had a little church fashion show. I wanted to be a model as well.

I ended up booking a huge modeling campaign that came out of New York City, and that prompted me to move there at 19 years old as a young Black model in New York City by myself. I always knew I was going to be in New York City just from my teen magazine days, where I used to read these teen magazines and they used to have these model searches to win a huge box of products. If you could get your picture posted in the magazine, you could win. I filled out all these postcards to make sure that I was going to win.

So I just always wanted to be this model in New York City, and it actually ended up happening from a campaign I booked. I was always doing auditions, and I wanted to look cute in my Polaroid photos. (This was before digital, before Instagram and Facebook.) I used to cut up lashes and place them on my eyelids. I would go to auditions and the other girls would say who does your makeup? Who does your hair? I would invite them to come to my kitchen, and I would do their makeup and hair. One thing led to another, where I had Brandy and Serena Williams come into my kitchen to get their eyelashes done. That's how I kind of got started creating D'Lashes. I used to call them extended wear lashes, then eyelash extensions, as everyone knows them today.

Kendra: I mean, some people say, "Oh, I want to be in the teen model search," or "I want to do this," and they may fill out one application here and again. But you were filling out hundreds of applications and said, "I am going to manifest this" and you did. You became the model you always wanted to become and then you pivoted. What was that

(continued)

transition like to say, "Okay, I'm going to go from being in front to now being behind the camera as an artist"?

Dionne: Well, I got tired of chasing an audition all the time. I worked as a model, and I literally worked all over the world. I've also done so many different things behind the scenes without really being known. Ultimately, I just really got tired of just chasing auditions. I love the joy of actually giving to someone and adding value to their lives. When I saw that joy after I applied eyelashes and did hair, that's what gave me the go-ahead to transition to behind the scenes.

Kendra: Interesting because we're always looking for something, right? We get it and something else drops into our life right at a divine moment. If we're open to receiving it, then we have this expanded life, and even more opportunities.

Dionne: I'm inspired to just be better than I was yesterday. I said yes to everything, which I've been doing since I was little, saying yes until I can't say yes anymore.

When building my lash products, I see what people are needing right now and just solve that problem for everyone. During this time of COVID, all of us were wearing masks, so the focus has been on our eyes. That was the answer for me to fill everyone's needs and what they wanted. They wanted something really natural. You can't have anything too big and too long because you have this mask on already that's constricting our breathing at the time. However, the market tells me what is needed. I listen to my clients. That's very important. When they come in, they tell me they want them longer over here, they want them shorter here, or whatever it is. And I listen to that.

That helps me create my lash line and also just to be aware of the needs of my clients in the market.

Kendra: Well, it's good because a lot of our founders talk about how they learn so much about their companies from listening. They may have had one idea, but when they started taking it beyond themselves and listening to the market, and, more importantly, listening to the clients, they had more success.

Dionne: The reality is that you attract who you are. Being in this industry, I definitely attract a lot of amazing insightful people.

Kendra: One of the things I love about being an entrepreneur and running my own agency is exactly what you said about attracting who you are. We get to carve out who we want to work with and we can say in order to do business together, we have a shared positive energy and approach to doing what is right.

Dionne: I think this generation has to understand that you have to have consistency in remembering why you're doing it and not just doing it for the celebrity aspect of it because it will never happen. You have to carve out what is important and remember that.

This is where self-actualization forms into a healthy, evolved ego. Self-actualization is the intentional conscientious acknowledgment of what you are good at, what you are not good at, what fuels your creativity, and ultimately what allows your best characteristics to fully bloom. Sometimes it can be hard to put a mirror up to yourself and realize you're not good at everything or even the things that you may have done to get by. Do not shy away from

(continued)

these traits or try to sugarcoat them. Be clear, be truthful, be humble. Self-actualization is the ultimate acknowledgment of humility, not self-loathing or projecting a lack of skill, but being clear and accurate. It also means knowing when you need to slow down, say no, and quite frankly just go to sleep. I think as entrepreneurs, we have to be able to say, yes, we are trying to move forward, but we're actually holding ourselves back. We need to have enough self-actualization to say, wait a second. It's hard when you're on this path and you're working so hard running full steam ahead to say, let me course correct, reflect, and try something that will serve me better and reward my strengths.

Take a few moments to dive deep into self-actualization. What did you uncover?

I excel at	I am good at	Not my strongest traits

Self-Actualization Across My Four Pillars

Community

Self-actualization expressed through my pillar of community means asking myself, "When do I need to be around others, and when do I need time to recharge by myself?" Sometimes in entrepreneurship, it is time to step away and breathe. That also means taking some time away from my husband, daughter, parents, and close friends. I am a firm believer in community to accomplish goals as well as taking a step away from the community to realign so that I can show up for the community in my best self.

Mentorship

Self-actualization for me around this pillar comes through the form of knowing when I need to be mentored, especially making sure I hold space and time for my executive coaching sessions, looking to others ahead of me, and saying I need to stop, listen, learn, and be mentored in this area of business and life. For all of us, it's acknowledging when we need support, a sponsor, a mentor, or even a coach. This awareness comes from looking deeply at and deconstructing what your lived experience has shown you thus far. Seeing where your shortcomings can be roadblocks to forward motion and success.

One important note is not to overthink mentorship. It doesn't have to be a weekly two-hour session with the CEO of a *Fortune* 500 company. More often than not, executives only have so much extra time to lend an ear or offer words of advice. Sometimes a quick call around a specific issue you are facing or an email with a list of questions can also provide support or a different perspective. Don't be discouraged if you DM someone and they don't immediately get back to you. Part of self-actualization is acknowledging that you may not be the most important thing in someone else's life. Being mindful of what's happening outside of your needs will help as you reach out.

Handy thoughts to keep in mind as a mentee:

- **Be direct in your ask:** What do you want and why?
- **What specific help they can provide:** Examples include an introduction to someone in their network, answering a specific question that they have experience in.
- **Do your homework:** Make sure that the person you are engaging has the experience that you are directly looking for; don't get caught up in titles, and research what they have actually done in their past career.
- **Be patient and know when to pivot:** Life happens, and sometimes the best intentions to provide mentorship or take a call can be derailed; be patient, give grace, and move on to someone else.
- **Be prepared:** When you finally get the person to engage with you, show up on time, have your notes ready, follow an agenda, and end the meeting on time.

Education

I love learning and being a student. I always try to educate myself on the potential outcomes surrounding the constant flow of ideas that I have before I execute, including who has done it before, whether it has worked or not, and what the potential metrics of success are. This step came after running far with ideas that were not sustainable or worth my time. As I started to reflect and write these experiences down, it was through self-actualization and silencing my ego that I was able to embrace letting some ideas go and not discarding others too soon. It was filters such as whether an idea aligns with my pillars and my time, or whether it would generate what I needed to be success-ful that I ultimately had to consider before moving forward.

At the beginning of 2022, I wrote down two key things I wanted to learn more about: venture capital (VC) and the metaverse.

Instead of stumbling around these areas, which are massive concepts, I let my guard down, asked for help, and surrounded myself with subject matter experts on each topic. In the venture capital area, I'm learning every day from my co-founder and chief investment officer, Lisa Stone, and our network of investors. I'm reading, I'm observing, and I am being educated at the grassroots level from organizations like the ILPA.org (Institutional Limited Partners Association). I joined BLCK VC and Visible Figures and surrounded myself with people like Kathryn Finney, who is the founder of Genius Guild, a venture capital firm.

To learn about the metaverse, I was so fortunate that I had Aisha Wynn, executive producer and blockchain expert, sit down on multiple occasions to educate me. I had enough awareness about my learning style and patience to know that articles and conferences were not going to be enough to get me the working knowledge I needed to truly conquer this goal. I had working educational sessions with founders on unit economics, what they want from investors, and how to innovate effectively; they educated me on dollars and sense.

The old cliché that knowledge is power is true; in fact, it's the greatest weapon a leader can have. Have enough self-actualization to know when you don't know something and be a knowledge seeker.

Join a class, free webinar, or attend a conference.

Read, read, read, and read some more.

Check your ego. You will never know everything, and you're never too old or too young to take the time to learn.

Find your community of experts: join LinkedIn groups, find local membership clubs, and identify professional organizations in your industry.

Talk, listen, talk, listen: let people know what you're trying to learn about, speak up as they may have knowledge you don't have or can introduce you to the right source of knowledge, and make sure to always be listening. You never know when something will be said that can educate you.

Capital

This is a tricky one because, as entrepreneurs, we believe our ideas will work and we will have the success we strive for. While I believe I am rooted in reality, I am constantly sitting in a state of self-actualization of when to stop a project, end a business, or pivot the business model to make money.

This pillar requires the most consistency, clarity, and the highest level of self-actualization. You need self-actualization and accountability to yourself and your business when it comes to capital, including financial, human, and social capital.

When it comes to financing your business, you don't want to give up too soon, but you also can't wait too long and miss the window of opportunity to raise money or even sell the business. Being forced to make decisions based on financial miscalculations is tough in any circumstance. When we think of human and social capital, both are much less tangible than the physical nature of the monetary funds, but they contribute in a very important way to the company's success and your own success as a leader. Human capital is the skills and abilities my team brings to business and social capital is the relationships we have with each other, including our individual responsibility to do things for and with others by offering access into our communities, networks, and resources. I want to build capital for my family, our founders, my community, and my team. This past year, I actualized what that looks like for me in the form of building the BrainTrust Fund to invest financial capital and BrainTrust Founders Studio to interconnect the importance of human and social capital working together to create an ecosystem of winning for underrepresented founders.

Sometimes you may be triggered specifically by conversations around financial capital, knowing yourself and being honest about the role money plays, from personal living expenses to bootstrapping and funding your own business to deciding which journey is right for you; you must do the work to have clarity around decisions you make, risks you take, and the path you chart for yourself.

> "My story is to inspire the world. I fundamentally believe God put me on this earth to inspire the world. I feel that in my being. I'm a giver, and I fundamentally believe that I am a man of service. I think we all, as people, this is just my opinion, we have to all get back to being of service. We all want to take and never give. I fundamentally believe that it's important to give first and your blessings will come."
>
> —Troy Alexander, founder, Troy Skincare

5 | Claim the Nonnegotiables

Do what you love, do what you want, follow your passion.
—Joni Odum, CEO, Firstline Brands

In 2018, when I was preparing to leave CAA-GBG, I was introduced to an amazingly talented businesswoman who had built a leading beauty and wellness incubator. During this period of transition, we spent months talking about how our businesses could support and benefit each other.

She was giving with her time and suggested that I take a Culture Index Survey (aka CI). While we ultimately remained friends rather than business colleagues, this simple survey became a window into my soul and for the first time provided clarity on the duality I was experiencing as an entrepreneur with an intrapreneur's robe on and the impact it was having on my true ability to fulfill my passion and live out my dreams.

It was through this CI process that I first set my nonnegotiables, which have guided me throughout my journey.

Culture Index Helps Business Achieve Greatness Through Their People

Originally born out of an inherent desire to help people achieve greatness like they never knew they could, Culture Index has become an integral business strategy for over 3,500 business leaders across virtually every industry. Today, Cecilia Bruening-Walstrom is the CEO and sole shareholder of Culture Index, making it the largest and fastest-growing female-owned and -operated strategic assessment business advising corporations everywhere.

CultureIndex.com, edited for print

Understanding Your Traits as an Intrapreneur and an Entrepreneur: Are They Different?

According to the introduction on the CI website, your individual CI is based on traits, a summary of seven work-related characteristics. These traits assess who you are outside of work, in other words, who you are when you are not modifying your behavior to meet the needs of your surroundings. These seven work-related traits are inherent behaviors and are typically established by ages 8–12.

The "Traits" summary of the CI helps you understand how you make decisions, what your communication style is like, the pace of the work you engage in naturally, and your inclination toward detail orientation or conformity.

The second section of the CI is entitled "Job Behaviors" and summarizes how you perceive you must behave to meet the demands of your existing job and the responsibilities you are accountable for. This summary may also be helpful in assisting you and other people as to the cause and/or effect of stress or possible morale issues, if prevalent, according to the CI.

My CI showed me who I was in my natural state, an entrepreneur, and who I was moonlighting as, an intrapreneur.

According to my CI, I am a logical person who perceives a need to react more emotively at work and show more sensitivity, typically because of the need to deal with a variety of people and their personal situations. As an intrapreneur, you are managing up, managing down, across, sideways, and horizontally to push your agenda forward. As an entrepreneur, my CI told a different story: "This person does not easily share their feelings and prefers to think with their head, rather than with their heart. Their detachment from events does not mean they are unaware of events or others' feelings. They are distancing themselves from the distraction of emotions in order to think more clearly."

In my role at CAA-GBG, I was an intrapreneur on the outside and an entrepreneur on the inside. According to my CI, "They are capable of stretching themselves out of character for short periods, but longer periods of behavior modification, especially where multiple stressors are prevalent, may tire this individual."

CI Summary

Here is an excerpt of my CI report.

Traits Summary

Naturally decisive, this person is aware of the issues at hand without being overly concerned for the specific problems. This problem solver is happy taking on potentially risky situations and conquering them. Will expect latitude and authority when taking on obstacles and does not willingly accept no as an answer.

This individual is analytically and socially inclined. They enjoy technical problem solving, but may delegate issues in order to spend time with people. Their communication style is coercive and, at times, persuasive and dynamic.

This person is opinionated, but is willing to compromise, especially in group efforts. Collaboration is important, and this reliance on social skills is balanced by their understanding of the situation. This person likes to initiate and finish activities in quick succession. They prefer variety in their circumstances and like working under pressure and time constraints. Forcing them into positions requiring methodical behavior is likely to induce disruptive behavior.

This individual is very effective when provided with, or allowed to set, priorities. They enjoy trouble shooting and then moving on. This individual wants problems to solve and may create one in order to have work. Assertive and visionary, this person is decisive and can accept responsibility for their actions.

This is a pleasant person whose communication revolves around persuasion and general concepts, although they are capable of using specifics if necessary.

This person likes variation in their work, but is capable of focusing on redundant tasks for short periods of time without losing interest.

This person may seem compliant in most situations but is capable of exhibiting more expeditious behavior when implied from the work assigned.

Resists structure or monitoring and assumes the ability to prioritize their workday. This person may demand details be finished in a certain way, but may require someone else to accomplish the task.

Potentially stubborn, this person focuses on personal interests and resists things that get in the way of their agenda.

Prefers a loosely formed environment and may become restless and disruptive under too much structure.

Tasks of low interest may be ignored in favor of a personal agenda. This person can delegate detail-oriented tasks.

An average amount of behavioral flexibility, this person may gravitate to positions requiring their specific skills and traits. They are capable of stretching themselves out of character for short periods, but longer periods of behavior modification, especially where multiple stressors are prevalent, may tire this individual.

This person does not easily share their feelings and prefers to think with their head, rather than with their heart. Their detachment from events does not mean they are unaware of events or others' feelings. They are distancing themselves from the distraction of emotions in order to think more clearly.

Capable of employing imaginative thought to situations, this person is open to new concepts and processes. They should be encouraged in this ability as they may otherwise rely on clichéd or habitual responses. Ingenuity is enhanced by experience and education.

Job Behavior Summary

Although they are naturally persuasive, this person perceives a greater need for enhanced social skills within the work environment. They recognize the need to increase their naturally expressive behavior; possibly to increase sales or interpersonal reactions among others.

The position is perceived as requiring quick responses to change and pressure and the ability to handle multiple tasks at one time. These requirements correspond with this individual's basic traits.

Due to the work culture, stronger attention to detail and greater follow through are perceived as a necessity in this position. The position is regarded as requiring an increased degree of structure, procedure, and compliance in the work assignments. This can also signify a greater need for accuracy and for taking a conservative approach to those same work assignments.

This individual perceives the need to be much more detail oriented and precise in their work assignments. This is typical of someone who also must be very concerned about the accuracy, specificity, and finiteness of their work activities.

This person feels a need to exhibit a greater than normal amount of behavioral flexibility, adaptability, and energy within their work culture.

This individual perceives the need to take on a greater than average amount of ingenuity to work and work culture. This person may be trying to use a more creative thought process or attempt to experiment with new products, or systems.

This is a logical person, who perceives a need to react more emotively at work and show more sensitivity, typically because of the need to deal with a variety of people and their personal situations.

Copy from Kendra's personalized CI report, edited for print

There are innate characteristics and traits that intrapreneurs and entrepreneurs have instinctively. I was in a conversation with Chidinma Asonye, COO of S by Serena, who summed up an interesting mindset and perspective around the need for founders and operators and the traits they each process.

I think right now, entrepreneurship and founding a brand feels very hot and sexy. I have so much respect for founders. I know that's not necessarily my skill set. That is not my ministry. I used to wonder, is there a place for me in this industry if I don't have this idea that I'm thinking, or I have an idea and now I'm going to get funding and I'm going start up the brand? No. Not for me. You also need people who enhance those people as well that are complementary. For me as a COO and really having a true executional skill set that someone who's an ideas person might be like, I love coming up with new ideas and then handing them off. I need someone who's going to build them out and really execute them and build a team to execute them. I think another thing for people listening to this is just thinking about what are your potential places in this industry if you're interested in beauty. It's not always just being a founder. I think sometimes there's this glorification of founders. By the way, that role is also really tough. There is founder fatigue and there are so many unique skill sets that I think founders need to have in terms of their ingenuity and in terms of their ability to see trends way before anyone even sees the value there, that it's very different than what someone who might be really executional might be good at."

—*Chidinma Asonye, COO of S by Serena*

Through multiple conversations, my own experience, and diving deeper into the results of my CI, I found that there is a set of characteristics that seem to appear across the spectrum of entrepreneurs and intrapreneurs—ultimately, the traits of leaders.

1. Courage
2. Fearlessness
3. Flexibility
4. Integrity
5. Ability to think outside the box
6. Strategic
7. Innovative
8. Go-getter
9. Effective
10. Game-changer

What I learned from this step on the journey as an intrapreneur in transition, leaving a corporate role and diving back into the world of entrepreneurship, was to claim my nonnegotiables and proudly lean into my traits and innate characteristics.

Leaning into Divine Epiphanies

Everyone's nonnegotiables will be different, and you should work to figure out your own. Sometimes a CI will help, and other times you might need a more drastic action like booking a trip to paradise and having an epiphany while paragliding over the favelas. That's when it happened to Natasha Edwards, who founded Thick Leave In after heeding an internal call to leave her career in medical ophthalmology and pursue a different journey. This led her to leaning into her divine epiphanies and claiming her nonnegotiables: peace, purpose, and honoring community.

Business of the Beat Excerpt, in Conversation with Natasha Edwards, Founder, Thick Leave In

Season 2, Episode 16, May 15, 2022

edited for print

Kendra Bracken-Ferguson
Podcast Host

Natasha Edwards
Founder, THICK leave-in

THE JOURNEY TO PEACE, PURPOSE AND COMMUNITY

Kendra: Natasha, your journey into entrepreneurship is such an example of following your inner self and claiming your nonnegotiables.

(continued)

Natasha: Prior to launching, I was actually working in medical ophthalmology. So I'm actually a surgical optimal technician. That is my background. So assisting the surgeons with retinal stand, assisting with cataract lens measurements, passing the instruments to the surgeon during surgery, like you name it, that is what I did for years. And it's not that I left because I didn't enjoy what I was doing. I left because there was a call for community. There was just something within me saying that what you're doing is great and you are working within the community in a sense, but you need to dive deeper and you need to serve the community on a deeper basis. So I actually quit in 2019, a few months before the pandemic. I listened to that inner guide.

The universe was just speaking to me, and I wasn't really sure what I wanted to do, but I knew I wanted to do something in community. I really wanted to take that time and have a break. So I went to Brazil. It was absolutely beautiful. I was able to really sit with myself and build with others that were there and network. It was an amazing opportunity. When I came back, I said, "Okay, I'm going to start a business, and it's going to be centered around community, but it's going to be an actual product that's tangible because it was very important for me to dive into something that I was passionate about." And then the pandemic hit in March, but I was already working with chemists and building out the product, and we were able to launch in 2020. I haven't looked back since.

Kendra: Congratulations. You are a true testament of listening to your gut and intuition. We all have it, but we have to be able to unlock it. My bishop says when it comes to your gut, faith, and intuition that if you wait too long to act once you feel or hear it, it starts to get quieter and quieter until it's gone. And it's not to say that you can never get it back, but it's about acting when you get it. I admire your courage to say, I'm going to leave. What was that like for you? You're in the medical field, and then you say, okay, I'm listening. And then you leave and spontaneously go to Brazil. What was that transition like in that moment in between when you felt it and when you left?

Natasha: The moment just felt right deep within. And I had to listen to that call. I really just quit, essentially. I walked in, I had a pair of shoes that were just there on the stand, and I made sure to pick up my belongings, and I just quietly left. My goal is to give two weeks. I'm very good that way. But that's how it happened. And when I left, I felt at peace. And the interesting thing is while I was there, while I was in the field, I absolutely loved my job. You know, some people quit because they just don't know what they're doing, or they feel like they're just on this grind. I was just loving what I was doing. I loved seeing patients and interacting with the surgeons.

But it was just time. It was more a personal decision for me. I had peace when I left, because I was at peace with my decision. And then going to Brazil just really put me in a good place to think of creative ways that I could really launch and really help others. And also, when you're in Brazil or if you're in a third-world country, a lot of things are being placed into perspective for your own life, like where you're at and how lucky you are and how you're able to serve the community. So being there was really helpful as well.

Kendra: You talk about this notion of peace, finding peace and finding center and the connectivity of it all. You said, I would usually give two weeks, which is standard, but

(continued)

when things aren't standard and things are rooted in faith and intuition, sometimes you just have to grab your shoes and make a change. I've been to Brazil too, and I agree it gives you perspective and reminds you to live in gratitude every day. When you get there and you see the difference, you're really pushed into a new state of gratitude. So why Brazil?

Natasha: My phone, funny enough. After I quit, I came home and was sitting on the couch scrolling through social media. In hindsight this was very kismet, like, the universe was talking to me, showing me things, just putting it in front of my face. I scrolled over a travel group talking about an upcoming trip to Brazil and the opportunity to learn about the community and history. I kept diving deeper, went on their website, and decided I was going to go. None of this was planned. I quit and figured I would go to the park or maybe just take a walk around the neighborhood and relax at home, but this trip to Brazil was something I knew I had to do. That was the moment, and the inner conversation I had with God was beyond belief.

Kendra: Your decision to quit and then go to Brazil takes so much courage and bravery. What were the three key takeaways from the whole experience and the impact it had on you that have reshaped the way that you look at the future?

Natasha: Number one, I would say the importance of community building. Number two is being grateful— being grateful for every moment, every opportunity, every interaction. Number three is just the importance of service. How can you use your gems and gifts to service others? And especially focusing on a local level and then expanding outside of that to see how it can become bigger and grow and flourish. Those are my three takeaways.

Natasha quit, listened to her gut, and knew it was time to connect her passion for community and product to start her entrepreneur journey.

What I learned about myself through my CI, coupled with my conversation with Natasha, was that my mission was to be my true self and not a version of myself. As my true self, I connected my pillars of community, mentorship, and education. Community through my team and protecting them even while unlocking my nonnegotiables as their leader—to lead on my terms and not under the guise of a system that fundamentally could not support our work. Mentorship from my boss when forced to say it wasn't working and to talk about the hard things while acknowledging how the best intentions sometimes don't work even when you want them to. Education about myself through my CI that shined a light on how I was altering myself, relinquishing my power, and not keeping my commitment to my nonnegotiables.

FAST COMPANY

03-14-22 | STRONG FEMALE LEAD

Corporate America spawned the fastest-growing group of entrepreneurs: Black women (but not for a good reason)

Global DEI thought leader Wema Hoover reflects on how the so-called leadership pipeline for Black women in corporate America takes them exactly nowhere. 'In fact, it practically buries them alive,' she says.

(continued)

It should not be surprising, then, that Black women are the fastest-growing group of entrepreneurs, with 17% in the process of starting or running new businesses (versus 10% of white women and 15% of white men), according to research published in *Harvard Business Review*. Why is that? In a nutshell, they're exhausted. They're exhausted mentally and emotionally from hitting their heads—not on a glass ceiling, but one as persistently impenetrable as concrete.

The truth is that Black women in corporate culture work 30% to 40% harder than their white male and female counterparts to get the same results—and that's if they're lucky. More often than not (as the research shows), the upward mobility that comes with experience, skill, and hard work is not granted to Black women. The so-called leadership pipeline for Black women takes them exactly nowhere. In fact, it practically buries them alive.

Black women who do succeed do so with great sacrifice that has an ill effect on their personal and family lives, their self-esteem, and their health. This is why they are taking their skills and passion and going elsewhere.

Fast Company, March 14, 2022

When I think about Black women in corporate America and my own experience as an intrapreneur at three of the largest companies in North America, I am further reminded to stay close to my nonnegotiables and my pillars as my foundation of growth and progress.

I encourage you to outline your nonnegotiables, take your CI, and unlock what you may be missing or hiding to fit in or exist in what seems comfortable. As Natasha said, she loved her job, but it was time to leave. Sometimes love is masked in ease and complacency, but when we listen to our gut, have faith, and are open to other experiences, we can unlock something we may never have imagined.

Spirituality Is Essence

> While Black women are the backbone of society in every facet imaginable they and their achievements continue to be marginalized. They have been the anchor and an ally of every important moment of transformational social change from the Civil War through today.
>
> —Marcus Glover, general and managing
> partner, Lockstep Partners

Tai Beauchamp, one of my lifelong friends, claims her nonnegotiables every morning on her show *Morning Mindset*. She took time to join me on season 1 of *Business of the Beat* to talk intimately about her journey. In 2004, Beauchamp became the youngest and first African American appointed to the role of beauty and fitness director at *Seventeen* magazine. She began her editorial career at *Good Housekeeping* and *Harper's Bazaar* magazines and went on to work as a beauty editor at *O, The Oprah Magazine*, and *Suede*, before joining *Seventeen*. She later moved into TV hosting, journalism, entrepreneurship, and so much more. During our conversation, we discussed how spirituality has played a role in our success and how she dives into its role in helping her be grounded and focused.

Spirituality, as Tai shares, is essential; it serves as a guide for her in all of her endeavors, including her businesses, relationships, and wellness. She believes that we are all given abundance and power but also need to tap into something greater in order to be successful. Tai claims her nonnegotiables—spirit, love, wellness, self-care, connecting with her tribe—as reminders of who she is as an individual.

Tai shares the journey of joining her co-founders, Malaika Jones and Nia Jones, to launch Brown Girl Jane, her mission, and why it is so important to connect with women. Finally, Tai dives into her thoughts on creating a brand that connects with its consumers authentically.

"Gratitude and expectations can and should always coexist." Tai explains that this is important for entrepreneurs because it allows them to be grateful for what they have while also demanding what they deserve. She added that this is especially important for Black women, who often face greater obstacles in business.

Business of the Beat Excerpt, in Conversation with Tai Beauchamp

Season 1, Episode 35, August 8, 2021

edited for print

Kendra: We've been together for almost 20 years, going all the way back to New York. So it means so much in this moment and this space to have made it this far and have you acknowledge the work that I'm doing, because I am just so inspired by the work that you're doing, and it takes all of us collectively to constantly keep acknowledging each other. You have always been so supportive.

Tai: Thank you so much, Kendra. And it's just a love for us because we have been together as friends since 2001 or 2002. You do know the journey, and I'm so grateful and I'm so proud of you as well, because we have had so many iterations of what it means to grow and to evolve but, most

(continued)

importantly, to build into impact. So I'm grateful for that. I started my career in magazine publishing more than 22 years ago now. I started really as doe-eyed, enthusiastic, always connected to humanity, but working in beauty, not knowing what the opportunity really would be.

I remember being this little girl, loving fashion and loving magazines and loving beauty, but never thinking that was something or an industry for me. And so I've just been really fortunate to have that legacy. Working on *Oprah*, *Seventeen*, *Harper's Bazaar*, *Vibe Vixen*, *InStyle*, and then going into philanthropy and working with my mentor and advising his family office on investing social impact, investing in Africa and in Newark, New Jersey, which is my hometown. And then I started my company by accident, but with intention, where I started consulting with brands and helping them to sell more meaningful and impactful brand narratives, really drawing on my experience as an editor and I think foundationally rooted in helping to empower women, which I learned from the best of Oprah Winfrey.

That led to, as I was working and consulting with brands, brands starting to say, we want you to be the face of the brand. Quite honestly, I was happy being an editor and being behind the scenes and helping to orchestrate and direct narratives and engage women in a meaningful way. But as God would have it, I was able to tap into a natural talent and skill set by engaging with people and started to appear in front of the camera. So fast-forward. I still do all of that with Tai Life Media, which you know very well because we have the opportunity to work together over the course of some years, intimately. And then I reconnected with college friends and now my co-founders,

Malaika and Nia, biological sisters, around Brown Girl Jane, which they had just started to work on.

They were saying, What are your thoughts? You're a beauty and wellness expert. What do you think about this? What do you think about CBD? What do you think about plant-based wellness? And I said to them, I think this is definitely something that is powerful. When I tried the product that was then in beta and early formulations, it changed my life, and I wanted to continue to evangelize the plant and wellness for Black and Brown women, especially because that's how I try and live.

Kendra: When you talk about Tai Life Media and Brown Girl Jane, both are rooted in this notion of God and being. On *Morning Mindset* this morning, you said, the spirit is what holds and shines a light on our physical being. So tell me about spirituality in terms of your journey.

Tai: I believe that we all have encounters with Spirit. People call it different things, and I appreciate that fully. I say that from a place of true belief. I grew up in a Christian household. I went to a Catholic school. My uncle is Muslim. My sister, who is my half sister, her mother is Jewish. She's Jewish. I've been exposed to all these faiths. So when I talk about Spirit, I think it's really important, especially as we talk about wellness, our being and that we all recognize that there is a spirit guide. There is a divine and divinity in all of us, no matter how you see it or how you decide to define it for yourself.

But I think as you grow in wisdom, you realize that you are given abundance and power, but you also can't do it alone. So there is something bigger at work that you have to tap into, especially when you don't have strength,

(continued)

especially when you don't know. And if, as you said, as we know it, this last year for all of us has been a year of reckoning, a year of consciousness, a year of leveling, a year of recognizing that there is something in and through us. There is a through line that is more palatable, not because of geography, but because of soul, center, and spirit. And so Spirit serves as a guide for me. Spirit serves as a guide for me in my businesses. It serves as a guide for me in my relationship. It serves as a guide for me in how I choose to grow, how I spend my time. And I think that the more we're willing to have conversations that don't seem so specific or so contrived and so forth, the more we will see expansion individually and collectively as a people.

Kendra: I love that. It's about how as a community do we come together? How do we recognize that there is something far greater than all of us, and especially individually, and that I truly believe, like you, there has to be a defined power that is guiding all of us because we can't do it on our own. Like, as much as we try and even as entrepreneurs, we try to carry the weight of so much to protect those around us, to protect our team.

But we also have to ground ourselves in knowing that there is something greater that exists, and to your point, whatever that is, and having the ability to be around all the different religions and spirit led, spirit-driven, spirit-blessed people, I think it really is powerful, and I can feel it radiate through you.

Tai: I am a believer. I think it's very important, as you know, we're talking about spirit, that people know that I'm a believer in God, creator, divine, but I'm also a believer in people. I'm a believer in humanity. I'm a believer in women.

I am a lover of people. I'm a lover of God, and I am someone's lover. So I am a founder of beautiful things that believe in humanity and the goodness of women.

I am a champion of other people. I'm a champion of the goodness that I see in people. I'm a champion of love. I'm definitely a champion full stop.

And to speak to people who are thinking about building a business or starting something, think about what is essential to and for you and use that as the blueprint or at least the informant of how you build. Because if something is essential to you, then you can make the case for how it can be essential to other people.

Kendra: When we think about being an entrepreneur, being a founder, it is that everyday grind that we get caught up in that it sometimes takes us away from the brand that we're building, the passion that got us there in the first place. We lose sight of our nonnegotiables and our own guiding pillars.

Tai: Yes, people who know me know that I prioritize self-care. It's a nonnegotiable for me. I've learned that if I don't prioritize self-care and practice what we preach at Brown Girl Jane, then a lot of things will fall through the cracks.

What we do is really focus on connecting with the tribe. While we center the needs of Black and Brown women unapologetically, we also have incredible women of all types who celebrate and support our product and our collection. And we're grateful for that. We want that because it is humanizing. So I think over the last year, from a business standpoint, I've learned to stay grounded and stay connected.

(continued)

Black and Brown female entrepreneurs are the fastest and largest demographic of entrepreneurs from a segment standpoint here in the United States. We have been taught humility as a people. And I appreciate humility. I think that there is a place for humility, and I think there's a place for reverence, of honoring and respecting the grace that has been afforded us. I do think oftentimes we stand in this space of humility to the detriment of knowing what we deserve and demanding what we deserve.

I say to an entrepreneur that if you're going in and you're seeking funding, don't be little in what you ask for, if you know you actually deserve the most. What we do is we challenge other people to recognize and to reckon with what we know to be true. And so you can be grateful to be in the room pitching, but do so with authority and say, I demand this because I know I deserve this.

And so we have to be very intentional about recognizing that while we're grateful to be in the space, we deserve to be in the space. You have to show up with that ownership. Coexisting is a recognition that it's deserving. We can be grateful and still demand and be understanding about what we expect. And the two are not mutually exclusive. And so I tell people, because you worked with me, in business, it's always so interesting because I am this kind person, and I'm a person of spirit. But in business, I don't play, Kendra.

We go to God and we're like, thank you, God. Thank you, God. Thank you, God. Thank you, God. And I believe that. Thank you, God. But also go to God with all of your expectations because abundance is meant for you.

Nonnegotiables Across My Pillars

We are greater than the data that constrains our character, our mindset, and how we approach life. The data may be a starting point for some, but we as people have to ultimately decide who we are going to be and what our nonnegotiables will encompass. I keep a framed note from my mom on my 30th birthday to remind myself that my nonnegotiable is being spiritually anchored.

> My dearest Kendra,
>
> Thank you for being my daughter and all the good and (sometimes challenging) experiences that you have provided. You represent the best part of my life. I thank God for you each and every day; I also pray for you to make wise decisions, to be spiritually anchored and that you know that you have a blessed life.
>
> May you remember this birthday and enjoy the life that God has allowed you to have.
>
> Delight in simple pleasures.
>
> Bits & Pieces:
>
> Life is a great big canvas; throw all the paint on it you can. Danny Kaye
>
> I have found if you love life, life will love you back. Arthur Rubinstein
>
> Character is doing what's right when nobody's looking. J.C. Watts, Jr.
>
> One never knows what each day will bring. The important thing is to be open and ready for it. Henry Moore
>
> With all my love
>
> 4/25/10

A framed note from my mom in 2010 on my 30th birthday to claim my nonnegotiable to be spiritually anchored

We must remain steadfast in the unique beauty and power of who we are. My nonnegotiables also show up in my four pillars across every aspect of my life.

Community

- My nonnegotiable: I will not be siloed or positioned against my community and my peers. No wall can divide what we are building together to change the future of economic advancement for underrepresented founders. I choose my brain trust every day.

Mentorship

- My nonnegotiable: I will not stop striving to deliver mentorship to my community, and I will never stop receiving the gifts and blessings of being mentored. You are never too high, mighty, or powerful to turn away mentors who seek to uplift and support you, and you can never be over mentored. The gift is understanding how to leverage and expand the knowledge that mentorship provides to progress you forward.

Education

- My nonnegotiable: I will not stop reading, learning, researching, asking questions, and being humble in my pursuit to learn more to be better. Education has to be a component to all I build, conceive, and focus my time on.

Capital

- My nonnegotiable: I will not stop pursuing prosperity and financial comfort for myself and others. God wants us to prosper. I will always be on the path to giving and receiving. *"To whom much is given, much will be required" (Luke 12:48)*. For me, this means we must take responsibility with a grateful humble heart for what we have and the blessings bestowed on us: wealth, knowledge, time, talents, and the like. It is essential that we benefit others.

6 | Protection

Today's Prayer: Father, I pray that You will be glorified and protect us as we move through this new season.

—Genesis 27:1–40

One of the pillars that I profoundly believe in and credit with so much of my success, with the doors opening and the opportunities that divinely entered my life at just the right time, stemmed from the protection that was wrapped around me in the form of mentorship. There is much to be said about mentors, champions, and sponsors, and I know firsthand the benefits of both at various stages of my career.

Former First Lady Michelle Obama says, "We should always have three friends in our lives—one who walks ahead, who we look up to and follow; one who walks beside us, who is with us every step of our journey; and then, one who we reach back for and bring along after we've cleared the way."

Over the years, I have been fortunate to have had people at each position: the one who walks ahead, the one who walks beside, and the one who I reach back to bring along. The beauty of this is that at any given moment, we may need a differentiated support system. I do believe that to stay humble, relevant, and in constant learning mode, you should always be able to identify and recognize those three people and thank them for the impact they have on your life. In writing this book, there are so many people who have filled these roles over the years, and I wanted to highlight three that instantly flooded my brain with memories, words, kindness, and trust. Since 2011, the person walking in front is Julie Flanders. Since 2003, DaVida Smith Baker has been beside me, and from 2018 to 2021, I brought Mitzi Aimee Gonzalez Flor along with me. (And the one person who has walked with me through all stages is my mother.)

Always manifesting, believing, praying, and supporting this journey, my executive coach, Julie Flanders, has been and will continue to be in front of me, steering me around sharp edges and introducing me to new concepts and parts of myself that I kept locked away, sometimes scared to dream as big as I could or even shrouded behind saying what I really meant.

Our relationship started with our first executive coaching session and me saying I wanted a lemon tree and a baby. That manifestation grew into a less-than-two-year time period of me and Pleas moving to LA, getting pregnant immediately, and renting our first house, which had a lemon tree squarely positioned in the backyard. It was also Julie to whom I finally released the anguish I had been holding in for my entire adult life around money and value. It is Julie who always connects the dots and holds space for my ideas, my mistakes, and my progress. While we have developed a personal friendship, we maintain our professional relationship with biweekly virtual coaching sessions, frequent in-person longer deep dives to focus on progression, challenges and wins, and consistent journaling. We have had many experiences together, and I will always keep her in front of me.

By profession, Julie is an executive coach, a Grammy-winning artist, a musician, a magical spirit fairy, and above all else my lifetime collaborator. I was the first one to initially steer clear of therapy, but I found that everyone needs some form of "therapy," whether it's through a spiritual leader, an executive coach, a mentor, and so on. Everyone needs someone who is close enough yet removed enough from the day-to-day to be a guide and to offer support.

Julie Flanders and Kendra, New York, March 2022

For me, I always wanted to separate executive coaching from psychotherapy or counseling, and I found that there will always be a convergence of the two, which for me takes the form of my life, my job, and my family all being rooted in FAITH and spiritual consciousness—because at any given moment, you favor one position in your life over the other. Success doesn't manifest in a bubble and we don't always know which way to go or which door to open. The right person in front of you can help see through the doors and up the mountain.

Standing next to me for more than 20 years has been DaVida Smith Baker, talent manager and producer at her own firm, Etcetera and Company. We met while I was in college at Purdue University and she was working in the athletic department.

DaVida and Kendra at Purdue University, Fall 2001

DaVida is a ride-or-die friend. She is a consistent voice, a steady presence, and a friend. She is a cheerleader and protector and has been with me at my highest highs and lowest lows. DaVida has saved me in business more times than I can count, always answers the phone, and always shows up.

In 2019, DaVida published *Sacred September*, a workbook created to help align your intentions to achieve your goals during the sacred month of September. According to DaVida, September possesses strong spiritual symbolism. While it's the ninth month in our calendar year, September gets its name because back in the day on the Roman calendar, September was actually the seventh month. Good ole lucky No. 7! She further defines September as a month to really connect with your goals as your Higher Power (I say God, The Universe, Source, and Higher Power) throughout the text.

I look back on the exercise outlined in week one (September 1–7) in the workbook, centered around connection. Each week you are encouraged to create an affirmation, a positive statement, to represent the theme that feels personal to you and your goals. Given the theme of connection, my affirmation for the week was "Lord, help me to discern what is for me and what is not." Throughout the month, this workbook reminded me to sit, connect to God, and navigate all that was revolving around me, some good for me and some not so good for me. I set my goals each week, determined my affirmations, and reflected on the challenges I needed to overcome to accomplish those goals. Ultimately, the core of cultivating protection is identifying who you can trust to connect with and bring into your brain trust. There is the authentic connection with Spirit and the chosen connections that we make that become essential in business, in friendships, and in all areas in which we interact with other people. To this day, my prayer is that God connects me to the right people, protects me from dangers seen and unseen, and wraps a hedge of protection around me and my family.

When I think about the great people I have had the privilege of mentoring, supporting, or even just giving a listening ear to, the person who stays on my mind constantly is Mitzi Aimee Gonzalez Flor, now a venture partner at United Talent Agency (UTA). I met Mitzi during our stint at CAA–GBG when Mitzi was an assistant to an executive who sat next door to me. When I suddenly found myself without an assistant, Mitzi raised her hand and said she wanted to move to my desk. She said she saw me constantly hustling, making moves, and always being in motion, and wanted to come and work for me.

Kendra and Mitzi, Los Angeles, February 2023

Mitzi is to this day one of the best employees I have ever had and someone I admire greatly. Mitzi always gave it to me straight and wasn't afraid to try her hardest at everything she set out to do. She stayed with me and helped mentor the team and be a voice when I couldn't speak at times. She started as my assistant and grew into so much more. I learned so much from Mitzi about my own leadership strengths and weaknesses, trusting my gut in taking chances, protecting my team, and the benefits of my unwavering loyalty for Mitzi and my team.

In a mentor-and-mentee relationship, there is so much give and receive everyday. Mitzi kept me on my toes when I was moving too fast to ensure flawless execution across the team, and spoke up when I was creating partnerships with external organizations that were too premature for my ambition. She protected me and I protected her. I gave her opportunities to excel, be visible, and grow in leadership. I coached her through difficult situations, and kept her by my side as I was navigating the transition from intrapreneurship back to entrepreneurship. I saw Mitzi grow into an executive, honing and sharpening her leadership skills.

Letter from Mitzi

Hi Kendra,

This last week I was focusing on moving back to LA, and the weekend turned into an endless errands journey. I wanted to ensure this email was thoughtful enough to convey my feelings appropriately—so please bear with me as it's a big one . . .

(continued)

In many ways I feel like I am starting from the very beginning five years ago at CAA's mailroom, except this time I have a much clearer goal in my head and a lot of great experience.

You and your work are a source of inspiration, admiration, and drive for me. I have never met a woman so bold, fearless, and relentless to create the companies they want to work in, and I aspire to build and accomplish any percentage of what you have done.

I'm excited to build personal resources, networks, and learn business models to hopefully build something that is personal to me as you have done with Founders Studio. For now I will continue to build a foundation and knowledge base.

I am so thankful to you for always championing my growth, and hope we cross paths more and more as I navigate this journey! My goals terrify me—and I would have never gained the courage to try to reach them if it wasn't for you.

Mitzi A. Gonzalez Flor, September 12, 2022, edited for print

The importance of these three connections and creating an expanded brain trust will enable you to create your own barriers of protection. My brain trust is ever evolving and expanding. When you think of your own connections, who were your three today? I would encourage you to do the same exercise every six to eight months and see how your needs impact your three.

Having these three people in my life has guided me during the best and worst times of my professional career and also through my personal evolution as an intrapreneur and entrepreneur.

Who walks ahead of you who you look up to and follow?

_____

Who walks beside you who is with you every step of your journey?

_____

Who are you bringing along?

_____

She Walked Ahead of Me So I Could Walk Ahead of Others

I've met many amazing entrepreneurs, and one of the most brilliant ones is Lisa Price. In season 1 of the *Business of the Beat* podcast, I had the privilege of talking with Lisa, the pioneer of textured hair, about founding Carol's Daughter. Carol's Daughter Healthy Hair Butter is part of the cultural expressions exhibit and a Collection of the Smithsonian National Museum of African American History and Culture. We talked about the need to have foresight and insight to be successful in business while leaving her mark on history.

During the Obama Administration, Lisa was appointed to the National Women's Business Council, an independent source of advice and policy recommendations to the president, Congress, and the U.S. Small Business Administration on economic issues that face female business owners. Lisa mentors female entrepreneurs and works closely with an array of organizations to give back to the community. She is also the author of

Success Never Smelled So Sweet, a memoir that chronicles her transformation from a young Black woman deep in debt to the president of a paradigm-changing business.

Through it all, Lisa provides Black female entrepreneurs the opportunity to see the magic of possibilities they might never have imagined.

Business of the Beat Excerpt, in Conversation with Lisa Price

Season 1, Episode 18: April 11, 2021

edited for print

Kendra: How do we help build the foundation and create the path for these entrepreneurs building businesses now?

Lisa: I think we just keep doing what it is that we do, and we make sure that as founders, we make ourselves available to the people who are coming behind us and around us. And when people ask me to mentor, I do my best to do that as often as possible, but not so often that it then becomes not worth doing. I remember what it was like to be in business and not really have many people to talk to. I had one friend who did what I did, and she still does today, so many years later. She's been in business, I feel like nearly 40 years, but she's always made hair products and bath products and skin products with a very different approach from the way that I make them.

So we never really felt like each other's competition, even though there were some stores that sold both of us. She just had such a unique approach to how she made her products that was completely separate from what I did. But we had each other to talk to, and we had things about us that were similar. There weren't people that you could call up on the phone who knew what it was like to have a pot of sea moss soaking in their kitchen that they needed, especially 27 years ago. Maybe it would be a little bit more usual now because there are millions of people following Tabitha Brown, and she showed us how to make sea moss jelly. So there might be more people that are familiar with that process today, but 27 years ago, not at all.

It can feel like a lonely place when you're an entrepreneur, and then when you're an entrepreneur who's a woman

(*continued*)

and you're an entrepreneur who's a Black woman, [the group] gets smaller and smaller. But with social media before COVID when we had all of the different conferences and things that we could attend, it changed the dynamic. It gave us a community. It gave us people to talk to.

I think more of us sharing the journeys and peeling back the layers will show other people, oh, I don't have to be perfect to do this. I didn't have to have that particular education in order to do this. Oh, I didn't have to have a parent that left me an inheritance in order to do this.

Kendra: I think that's so true. And I want to even go further with that too, because even when we talk about communities and mentors, you are a mentor for BeautyUnited. When Moj (Moj Mahdara) and I created BeautyUnited, it was right at the beginning of COVID. I'll never forget being in the office on Friday and I said to Moj, I think we should close the office. Something's happening. And just like that COVID hit and we never went back to that office again. And then we started calling people in the industry to help each other to essentially unite and come together in an effort to support and seek answers together. It was through that time that we launched the first mentorship program with over 100 Black and Indigenous mentors and mentees, and you gave so much of your time to that program. It was so rewarding and we had so many founders say, I was able to raise money, I hired employees. COVID taught us that we have to make sure that we are supporting and showing up when it's good, but also when it's really hard.

One of the things that you've shared that I thought was just fascinating was that your mentors, while growing your business, were Martha Stewart, Oprah, and Goldie Hawn, but it was more about not trying to be them, but watching how they move.

That piece is crucial, especially when you talk about finding someone that you can talk to who's in a similar path. Having people like Oprah or Goldie to look at, but also saying, I'm still myself and I'm not going to be them, so how do I take their experiences, navigate them for myself, and kind of unlock what's going to work for me?

Lisa: Absolutely. I'm an introvert. And it would have been so challenging for me to walk up to a stranger and ask them to be my mentor. I don't think I could have done it. And I'm grateful for being able to learn from those people from a distance. It's not about trying to become Oprah, but it's about watching someone move authentically through their life and all the while growing and becoming more powerful, while sharing and giving back and never not helping, never not teaching, never losing sight of that.

Looking up to Lisa has offered a sense of protection to me. I've sat in the warmth of her kitchen over tea and had the honor of sharing our experiences around life, family, and business and the ultimate gift of joining her prayer circle. She reinforces the importance of my vision to support other Black founders by believing in and holding space around the phenomenal impact of uplifting, giving back, and creating a support system for the next generation of entrepreneurs who look like us.

I now pray daily for God to create a fortress of protection around not just me but the vision and the work we are putting into the world. For me, protection has multiple layers: protection of my peace, my family, my ideas, my team, my health, my work, my life. There are so many things I pray over and, as we all experience in life, all things are ultimately out of our control. We do our best. We surround ourselves with people who we know have our backs, and we keep our spiritual center centered.

Sometimes it's the small reminders of protection that we can't overlook as giving thanks for having a blessed protected life. Every time my daughter and I get a good parking spot, we give thanks to the parking angels who have protected our time looking for a spot and protected our walk to the door.

Today's Prayer: 1 John 4, 5
Father, I am grateful, and I thank You for keeping, protecting, and providing for me all year long. Would You please help me serve You well next year?

We must protect our energy and our space, and know that the ultimate outcome will be good. What God has for us, He has and we pray for protection. I have to continue to release this notion that I have to be on guard for the bad because I am getting something good.

For example, I remember telling myself early in my career that I had to stop going to church so the devil didn't catch wind of my success and then knock me down. It seemed like there was this point where the more I leaned into God, the harder life became, so I would skip church and try not to lean into faith. Looking back, I realized that with all things come both the good and the bad. It's the ebb and flow of life, and the true testament to faith and abundance is how you move yourself through it, meaning how you treat other people and stay steadfast in your faith. In those moments, we must say this too shall pass and hold onto our faith to persevere to our next chapter of life.

Protected by Angels, the Story of Troy Alexander

When it comes to protection, one of my most inspiring conversations was with Troy Alexander on season 2 of *Business of the Beat*.

Troy Alexander's light radiates as he walks into any room. Founder and CEO of TROY Skincare, a clean, premium men's skincare brand, Troy is the epitome of manifesting your dreams and purpose. He exudes confidence and humility and is an advocate for giving and community building. His LinkedIn profile reads "Disruptive Entrepreneur & Cultural Tastemaker." I'll add mentor, philanthropist, style guru, and a man of vision and service.

Troy got his start in the beauty industry as the digital face of Symrise, a fragrance house, where he also sat on the advisory board. He worked as a contributing columnist for prestigious publications including the *New York Times*, *Forbes*, and *Yahoo! Beauty* and has been featured in others like *Vogue*, *GQ*, *BloombergBusiness*, and more. Troy is uplifting and inspiring with his stories of his time in prison, his grounded faith, his take on multigenerational wealth, and centering patience as one of his pillars.

> [Prison] was the best thing that happened to me because that was my MBA . . . I learned a lot about myself and I became a better man, because I studied the men that were in there and the people that were in there. The same people that are in there are out here.
>
> —Troy Alexander

Business of the Beat Excerpt, in Conversation with Troy Alexander

Season 2, Episode 11, April 10, 2022

edited for print

Kendra Bracken-Ferguson
Podcast Host

Troy Alexander
Founder & CEO, Troy Skincare

LISTEN TO THIS EPISODE ON   Apple Podcasts   Spotify

Kendra: Troy, you are phenomenal. We've had conversations personally about your time in prison, how that motivated you, your vision to create TROY Skincare, and the lessons around protection, patience, and God as your center. Go back to the beginning and tell us your story.

Troy: Well, I had a really great childhood. My mother had me when she was very young. I think what I've learned in life is that when you have a single mother, and especially as a young boy who lacks a father, lots of things can happen. I think for me, it was a journey and a process through that. I recall many times, my stepfather, he would always say to me, one day you'll go to prison. I was like, What do you mean? He's like, one day you'll go to prison. Because he saw something. And sure enough, I sure did.

That was the greatest thing that happened to me because that was my MBA. I learned so much about myself. And I was so protected in there. I was a young kid. I didn't know what I didn't know. But, I learned a lot about myself, and I became a better man because I studied the men that were in there and the people that were in there, because the same people that are in there are out here. That's why I'm able to see so many different things and feel so many different things. Because if you see a man get sexually assaulted when you're a young kid, if you see gang rapes, you see so many things in that environment, and so it altered who I was.

And so I went to therapy. I saw a lot of things inside there that most people never see in their lifetime. I still struggle with a lot of things. I'm still in therapy because I want to keep getting better. I want to do better, get better, and be stronger. I think for me, that's what we need to all start doing. We need to start being better, getting stronger, and start loving ourselves. That's one of the most important things. Why I want to create TROY Skincare, because it was a transition for me. Prison taught me that I never wanted to work for anyone. At that early age, I wrote down everything that I've ever wanted to accomplish. I dreamt so big because you got to imagine: you are in this six-by-nine

(continued)

cell and you have a sliver of a window. I could predict when the time was.

I could predict if it was going to rain or whatever, because I kept studying. I was a student. What prison gave me was the opportunity to think. And, Emerson said this very incredibly. He said, What is the hardest thing for people to do? And it's to think. For two years, all I did was think. So I played chess in my head. I realized what I wanted to do, and I didn't care how long it took. I think so many times with my brand, everyone's like, launch your brand, launch brand. No, I have patience. And that's what prison taught me, patience. I'm not in a rush. That's the greatest gift that I have. And that's what prison taught me. I run my own race. I don't worry about what anyone else says.

Kendra: I'm overcome, overwhelmed with the emotion of everything that you said, the seriousness and the severity of things that you couldn't control. I think that no one leaves childhood unscarred. We have to figure out how to evolve as a person and move forward to reach your potential.

Your stepfather said, You're going to go to prison one day; that is where we understand and recognize the power of words and our power of language over others, and that we have to sow into ourselves, our children, our friends, our parents, whoever's around us in a positive way. Because you start to manifest those words. And to hear you say, you are going to be something different and do better is the counter to those words.

You mention God protecting you. Was your spirituality something that you developed in prison to protect yourself and to cope with what you were seeing? Or did you come in with spirituality? How did it alter your journey?

Troy: Growing up, my mother had me in church all the time, and I think that was the start of it. When I became a late teen, I was like, I don't care about that. When I went to prison, the greatest thing that happened to me there was this correctional officer. As I walked by, she said you don't belong here. She was so spiritual, and she was such an angel. She said that to me, and I said, What are you talking about? And she said, You don't belong here; God is going to protect you. I didn't know how to receive that. She said those words to me. And through the course of my journey, of those two years, I had cellmates that protected me, that watched over me, that schooled me. I was so incredibly blessed because I was a 20-year-old kid in prison with men.

The greatest thing that my cellmate told me was never tell anyone how much time you have in here, because it's easy to get in prison, but it's hard to get out. Any one of us can go to prison. You could be a drunk driver. You could have back child support. Anything can happen. And you can go to prison. If you have less time than someone else, they could run your time up. That's the difference when you get in there. It's easy to get in there, but hard to get out. He told me, tell everyone you have 33 years.

And that's what I did. That protected me. What people don't understand is that in life, you have to adjust to your situation. My faith came back to me because I realized that, Oh, I can go to church every day, and I can get out of this cell. I'm going to church every day. Sign me up. Great. I started to develop my spirituality even greater, and I leaned on that, and that was incredible for me because it saved my life. I was truly protected by angels.

(continued)

Think back to a protector in your life, an angel walking in the flesh who was vested enough to mentor, coach, champion, and create opportunities for you to shine.

How did that relationship impact your trajectory?

_____

_____

_____

_____

_____

We All Win Together

In 2021, I was asked to join the Toast to Equity summit hosted by *Forbes*. Who knew that this panel would lead to so many new relationships, including with Helen Aboah, chief executive officer of Urban Zen, a design vision and philosophy company founded by fashion icon Donna Karan?

Helen joined me on season 2 of the *Business of the Beat* podcast and inspired me to think back to a mentor in my life who was vested enough to coach me and create opportunities for me to shine. Helen had many mentors, but two women of color, in particular, stood out as early sponsors whom she credits with shifting her dynamic career. Helen's cross-industry career spans fashion, hospitality, health and wellness, and entertainment, with a deep foundation in the global luxury goods market across wholesale and retail (digital and physical channels).

From the time that Helen joined the executive team at LVMH, a French holding multinational corporation and conglomerate (formed by the merger of Louis Vuitton with Moët et Chandon and Hennessy) specializing in luxury goods, her journey through the creative side to merchandising product development strategies gave her the perspective and expertise to lead Urban Zen's iconic expansion globally.

Helen and I chatted about her vantage point as a Black female executive, her timely decision about motherhood, and the relevance of Black excellence in white spaces.

Business of the Beat **Excerpt, in Conversation with Helen Aboah, CEO, Urban Zen**

Season 2, Episode 13, April 24, 2022

edited for print

Kendra Bracken-Ferguson
Podcast Host

Helen Aboah
CEO, UrbanZen

LISTEN TO THIS EPISODE ON   Apple Podcasts   Spotify

Kendra: Helen, you are the CEO of Urban Zen, and as we were preparing for the show, we were trying to figure out how many women of color, in particular Black women, are CEOs of major luxury brands and were having a hard time. And you are one of few, if not the only.

Helen: Yes, I am, which is somewhat remarkable. It's something I hope to see that will be changing in the near future. I always reference these numbers that African Americans make up 14% of the population, yet less than 3% of senior managers or executives across all the industries. So as a Black female CEO of a luxury retailer, it's normal for me to be the only Black person, not just in this executive role, but sometimes even in the room.

Two of my mentors are Asian American women who have really shifted the trajectory of my career. Early on, they were not just mentors, but sponsors, and guided me along my career. So one of them was at Alexander Wang, and she had been brought on to lead the organization. And she said, Hey, can you come on board? We have this new strategy. And I think that you're the only person that can do this. So I went ahead and said yes. By the time I left, I was the chief merchandising officer and executive vice president, overseeing about 80% of the organization.

I felt like, wow, I could be doing more because of my role, and I started just being more conscious about the people around me, what they were strong at, what were they good at, how can I mentor and sponsor them, to grow them in their career, which I was very fortunate to do there.

And then some years later, Donna Karan, who I've known for a very long time, had been for some time trying to get me to come over and help expand and grow Urban Zen to new territories. As soon as I started, not even a few months later, COVID hit.

I thought, Oh my God, I just took on this big role. Now COVID is here. What am I going to do? I've always been agile, and we had a great team. I can't express enough the importance of leadership in the company, an advisory

(*continued*)

board, and people around you who make you feel safe and secure and doing your job.

I think about the former CEO of Disney, Bob Iger. In his book *The Ride of a Lifetime*, he credits his mentors because he said they gave him room to fail. Had they not, he would never have been the CEO of Disney. And having that space to not feel like, Oh, my God, if I mess this up, if I do this, my whole world is going to crumble. It's my reputation, it's the job, it's the companies, these employees. And then immediately with Donna, the board came around and said, Hey, look, we're here to help you carry this, and we're going to do this together, but you come to us with your strategy, and we're going to support you. We want you to win. The incredible board directors said, Look, nobody's going to get this 100% right. Because nobody has been here before or in this position before.

And at that moment, I immediately just said, You know what? I got this. We're going to figure this out. And we did.

Kendra: You've said it in a few different ways, that without people around you, you couldn't do it. You talked about being able to carry it forward and be successful because you have this amazing board, and you also talked about your two mentors.

So when we think about mentors and sponsors and building this team, what advice do you have for other leaders, founders building teams, to make sure that they can instill this sense of "we're in it together"?

Helen: That's such a good question for me. They were instrumental in providing me the career and professional advice that I needed. I would say to anybody who's looking to be an ally or assist or mentor or sponsor someone, it's that people do need help further developing and mapping out a career path that they want for themselves. We all have a sense that we know what we want; we just don't know how to get there. And that's where mentors and sponsors can come in and say, let's map that together. This is the development that you need to undertake to get there, be prepared for it. But they didn't just stop there; they also took the next step in advocating for me to get the promotions, raises, and even helped me land jobs in other companies, because they were vested.

For people who are looking to be allies and to be those mentors, you have to be vested. And if you're not vested, then I think it's the second step, because you've given someone maybe the tools, right, or the map, but they probably don't have the vehicle to get there. And you have to help by being that vehicle to get there, whether that's helping someone raise funds. Because recently somebody said to me, Oh, somebody told me I can go here to raise funds for my business. And I said, Okay, but how are you going to get through that door? Who's going to make the introduction for you?

And not only the introduction for you, but who's going to then speak about you in such a way that the person is going to want to open the door to speak for you or speak to you? And then for those who are looking for the mentors, I always say that not every mentor is going to be the CEO of your company. In my case, my immediate direct reports, sometimes they're a level two, they vary, but in general, it's these building blocks. So look for that person who is your manager, right, one step ahead of you, because you're just trying to get to the next step. If you're trying to

(continued)

go from A to Z overnight, that's a problem. And there's no mentor big enough who's going to help you get there responsibly.

Look for those people who can get you to that next step who are accessible to give that advice and guidance. And I can't stress how important it is because they were critical to my career. I can get emotional about it just because they were the ones when I was stuck were like, Look, you're stuck not because there's this glass ceiling. You're stuck because you need to develop in this area. In some cases, they were like, Oh, the reason that you're stuck is because you haven't had an opportunity like this.

A Reason, a Season, a Lifetime

It may sound clichéd, but I do believe that people come into your life in the form of angels to protect you for a reason, a season (an assignment, a mission), or maybe even for a lifetime. I count my "lifetimers" on less than two hands and know that in the end we'll be together. They are ever-present, and we don't expect much from each other on a day-to-day basis.

I can count my "season" friends on multiple hands, knowing that when the season rolls around, we'll make it happen. The hardest group for me to navigate is the "reason" friends . . . give, take, take, give relationships. There is an underlying tone with these friends in business, and you quickly know it's transactional the first time you say let's figure out how to help each other. This is tricky because sometimes "reason" friends stay there too long and quietly creep into seasonal friendships that honestly don't serve either of you well.

I have the gift of light, and the balance between friends is something I'm always navigating. When I think of protection, just like the friends who walk alongside you, next to you, and behind you, these seasonal friends can bring a layer of protection, mentorship, community, and education just when you need it the most. It's our ability to decipher and receive the gifts of each relationship that truly brings value.

> Dear Kendra,
>
> In every instance you've come away stronger but perhaps not in a lifelong relationship. So could it be you just need to let it be what it is. Not get caught up in the long-term feelings. Do what you need as always, and know that this relationship is for a reason to make your vision and passion a reality.
>
> This is what it's always been—use what God has put in front of you as a source of help to guide you to the next level of success that He has outlined for you.
>
> God has given you the best of the best always! Lean into it and release what's holding you back. It's only for a season of success for you. The lifetime is in accomplishing what you set out to do.
>
> Love, Julie Flanders (May 24, 2022)

Lean in and know that at any given moment, these friends may move into other positions to help you achieve your goals.

Dear God, Thank you for bringing angels into my life. Thank you for wrapping a hedge of protection around me and my family. Protect my team, our time, our work, and the community we serve. Amen.

7 | Jungle Gym versus a Ladder

Nothing is a failure but an opportunity to do something else.
—Bobbi Brown, professional make-up artist, author, founder
of Bobbi Brown Cosmetics, founder and CCO of Jones
Road Beauty, justBOBBI.com, and The George
(as shared at JP Morgan Chase Leadership
in Beauty Event, November 8, 2022)

You never know when someone will come into your life who will care as much as you do, stand for the same things you believe, and work just as hard as you to make them happen. These unexpected angels cause you to pinch yourself and say, Wait, we really are in this together. That's why my mom always says to me, "Treat people right. We never know who we'll meet along the journey, but we just treat everyone right."

I met Chidinma Asonye, COO of S by Serena, on a Beauty-United videoconference during COVID. We quickly connected offline as two of the few Black women to oversee and operate two of the most recognizable A-List Black female celebrities' companies. She was one of my first YESes when I asked her to join the advisory board of BrainTrust Founders Studio and later became an early investor in our BrainTrust Fund. Chidinma joined me to talk about will versus skill on season 1 of my podcast. She shared her journey from Wall Street to beauty to fashion and believes that there is not one right way to be a leader.

> "Your career is more of a jungle gym than a ladder."
> —Chidinma Asonye, COO of S by Serena

Business of the Beat Excerpt, in Conversation with Chidinma Asonye, COO of S by Serena

Season 1, Episode 19: April 18, 2021

edited for print

Kendra: Chidinma, you are the chief operating officer at S by Serena, a brand founded by Serena Williams that celebrates and empowers women to be seen and be heard. Prior to that, you were an executive at Estée Lauder, focused on global ecommerce, and prior to that part of the luxury fashion and beauty practice at Boston Consulting Group. You began your career in private equity and investment banking. Let's start there, from private equity and investment banking to fashion to now running such an amazing historic brand, talk about your journey.

Chidinma: In the beauty industry, I'm not sure how many people have come from Wall Street to beauty, but a mentor once told me that your career is more of a jungle gym than it is a ladder. When I first started on Wall Street, would I have expected myself to be a brand builder and working in the fashion, beauty, and wellness industry? I don't think so. One thing that I always think about is how nice it's been to actually authentically think about each step in my career and not necessarily have it all planned out. I think people are always saying, Oh, what do you want to be when you grow up? I wish people asked people that, not just when they were three or 10, but they asked them when they were 20 and when they were 40 and when they were 60.

Because I feel like there've been steps in my career where I took one big step up, but sometimes there was a doubt inside and sometimes a lateral move that I wasn't quite sure what would happen next. But it all sort of worked out. That's just something I encourage people to think about: to not be so linear in your thinking.

(continued)

Kendra: I love the notion that your career is more of a jungle gym than a ladder. That resonates with me so much because you're right, everyone is always asking, What's your five-year plan? Sometimes you kind of have to be where you are at that moment, and it may be lateral, it may be upward, but I think what I've really been looking at is, what am I passionate about? For you, did you find that you were passionate about banking and finance and that passion evolved into beauty? Was your skill set transferable?

Chidinma: I'm actually glad you brought up transferable skills because when I first started investment banking, one of my thoughts was that I really wanted to have a rigorous quantitative education, because I felt like in any career, you could use those skills. I actually was an economics major in undergrad, which I thought, well, how do you make money after you graduate from economics if you don't want to be an economics professor? Being in finance actually felt like a natural fit. I started to think about my career more as, What am I adding to my toolkit? What am I learning here? Also, what things am I learning that I dislike? That is another thing I think people can sometimes discount in a career path is that sometimes it's just as important to know what you don't want to do and what doesn't excite you—what doesn't drive you, what doesn't motivate you—just much as what does motivate you, because it helps you home in on that target of where you want to be.

What I loved about being on Wall Street was the rigor, the pace of the excitement, learning lots of different industries, doing something quantitative. I wasn't necessarily that passionate about finance. It's funny, I remember reading something that said you can tell when someone is in the flow on their job where things just come easy. I felt like there were people that I saw that were just living their best life every day as if they were just meant to be there. And that never felt like me. I was putting in the effort and getting the results, but I wasn't ever feeling like, yes, this is where I was meant to be until I was doing things that were more consumer and fashion focused. Actually, funny enough, when I first started thinking, oh, consumer businesses are so interesting; I love the psychology of people and connecting with people, I always felt like that was an underutilized part of my skill set. I actually questioned myself a lot, saying, well, is it because I'm a woman that I'm thinking like a shopping career or retail or fashion would be fun? I really discounted that love and not realizing actually how big and powerful and meaningful the beauty, fashion, and wellness industries are to women specifically, but just in general, to the economy.

Kendra: I like that you mention, is this passion for consumer goods and fashion because I am a woman? It's fascinating because one of the things that I'm focused on is changing the faces that we see at the top of these beauty and wellness brands, because there's a certain place where you see women and you see women of color, but you kind of get stagnant as you move to the top. That's because intuitively, we've been taught to think that as women like, you go do these certain jobs but you don't do these jobs or rise to the highest levels of leadership. We have to say, I can be passionate about it, and I can do this even if I'm a woman. There need to be more of us feeling confident in that right, to be able to explore all roles.

(continued)

Chidinma: One of the reasons why I love what you're doing [at *Business of the Beat*] is sometimes if you can't see it, you can't be it. There are certain industries, and I think of, like, the restaurant industry, where there's this stigma about women in the kitchen in this very domestic way. In many high-end restaurants, all the top chefs are men. Similarly, in the beauty industry, though, it's an industry that caters to women. When you look up so many of the *Fortune* 500 and even smaller-brand CEOs are men, and they're typically white men, there's not necessarily a ton of diversity. I think as you look up and you don't even realize how much that's impacting you of just not seeing folks who look like you in so many different ways, it can be hard to start to think about yourself in those roles.

Kendra: You have been successful in private equity and finance, where the roles of women and women of color are even less so. You have had to kind of navigate both industries to get to where you are now. How has that been as a woman, as a Black woman? Have you seen the shifts, or what shifts are you following?

Chidinma: One of the things that I feel like I was taught early on was that there's one way to be, so you should assimilate into the culture. In banking, you try to be as non-emotional as possible. You try to just be as much of a workhorse as possible. You don't show so much of your personality. I started to realize, you know what? That's a paradigm that doesn't necessarily work for me. How can I actually use my unique skill sets to bring something different to this job? What I realized was even just my ability to connect with people, whether that was senior managing directors or whether that was clients, that was actually a value. Once I actually started leaning into that and showing that skill set at work, it was really valuable. I think it separated me and differentiated me from my peers in a way of saying, okay, there's not just one good way to be a good banker or one good way to be an M&A or one way to be a leader.

When I transitioned into private equity, oftentimes you're sitting on the board level of companies. You come to company meetings, and they're often looking at you as an outsider and kind of thinking, What do you know about my business? Not really necessarily wanting to trust you. I started to hear feedback from people, that when I was around, "The company leaders open up to you" or "are more comfortable around you" or "You seem to get insights from people that we wouldn't otherwise get." I was starting to realize, that's my unique gift and skill. How can I actually apply that in a way that's not necessarily what the industry says, but is authentic to me? When I started doing that, I actually did start to feel that feeling of, oh, I can be in the flow here when I'm bringing my unique self and my unique gifts to it.

Kendra: I love that you say that, and I love how you also said understanding what our skill is, but then also understanding what you don't want to do. I think so many times it's like, well, this is what I want to do and also being very clear about what we don't want to do too, because that's how, to your point, we really get into this flow of figuring out our unique skills and gifts. It wasn't until after I started my first company, Digital Brand Architects, and working with my business partner that I even felt comfortable saying, this is what I'm good at. I'm good at building a brand. I'm

(continued)

good at navigating people, I'm good at building community, and so on. I think it's getting to a place where you can say that unapologetically.

I've literally had to do the exercise writing, "This is what I want to do. This is what I don't want to do. Does this position put me in a place where too much of what I don't want to do shows up?" Because I know I'm not going to survive. How did you get to that place where you're like, this is my unique skill, and I'm getting in the flow?

Chidinma: In some ways, I think being a Black woman in so many of these spaces (Michelle Obama has talked about it, too, about her experience at Princeton) is that the hardest part is actually getting in. When you get there, you realize you're no different than most of the people there. There's not something so special happening behind these closed doors. That, to me, was a big *aha* moment at Harvard Business School. Not that there weren't brilliant peers and people doing amazing things, but I think for me, the hardest part of the process is just the fact that the acceptance rate is so low. When I got there, I thought, What? I deserve to be here. I'm bringing just as much as some of these folks. There are actually so few Black women at HBS—less than 20 per year graduate from a class of over 900 people. It was a place where, actually, my unique perspective as a Black woman, I thought was really valued and needed.

I think that whole experience of getting my MBA at Harvard has shaped a lot of how I think about my career.

Figuring out why you're doing something, why you're going to school, why you're at this job, and why you are here is so important. Everyone has a unique path, and it's not right or wrong. Your career can be more of a jungle gym than a ladder.

Climbing Your Own Jungle Gym

In those moments of doubt, I go back to my conversation with Chidinma Asonye. People can be hurtful when they just don't understand or comprehend another person's path. When Jack Dorsey was the co-founder and CEO of Twitter, Inc., or when he was the co-founder and CEO and chairperson of Block, Inc., as well as the developer of the Square financial services platform at the same time, no one was constantly questioning his ability to do two jobs at once. When I was doing more than one job, I was told hundreds of times that I was doing too much or asked questions about how can I do this and that. It's been disguised in various ways: I've been told I have too much on my plate, that I am not focused enough, or that I shouldn't try to do too much, all while having business success. This white man ran two of the biggest companies at the same time and was praised and applauded.

I've known since kindergarten that I have a high capacity and high tolerance for work, developing big ideas and taking on projects. This capacity is one of my superpowers; however, I don't expect others to have the same capacity I do. We all contribute with our own gifts. When I get the comments, questions, or looks of disdain, I'm reminded of the jungle gym that I climb that fuels my energy, enables me to keep going, and reminds me that I'm not climbing a ladder. I'm on my own jungle gym of life.

What I mean by this is that your career does not have to follow a straight path in a way that others understand or even relate to. As Chidinma shared, you should figure out what you enjoy in each job so that you can figure out what your next move is, even if it's a lateral move or changing industries, as she did.

In fact, sometimes I have to keep much of myself and my desires to myself so that I am not cut off from my path by others before I even get started. Not everyone moves through life the way I do or the way you do. Getting to the top of the jungle gym is about mapping out your moves along the way. You might even get knocked off by life or by things you can't control, but continuing to climb will eventually get you there.

It's often said that no one makes it from childhood to adulthood unscarred. That may be true, but how do you overcome your trauma? How do you keep your momentum on the jungle gym versus sitting at the bottom? For me, the jungle gym metaphor is the same as my mantra "Carpe diem," or seize the day. Every day that we are blessed to wake up, we can start new. Every day, we can choose to climb or sit at the bottom. Sure, there are times when I want to sit at the bottom and I have to pull myself up inch by inch. We are human, and we have to give ourselves grace. Sometimes we climb, and some days we need to sit in order to be able to climb tomorrow.

Let's sit at the bottom of the jungle gym together and answer these questions:

What do you feel sitting at the bottom as others climb?

_____

_____

_____

_____

_____

Why are you sitting at the bottom?

_____

_____

_____

_____

_____

Why does climbing today seem so hard?

_____

_____

_____

_____

_____

What do you need to be able to climb that you don't have already?

_____

_____

_____

_____

_____

Are you satisfied sitting at the bottom?

_____

_____

_____

_____

_____

If you were climbing, would you climb straight up or move laterally to try that route?

_____

_____

_____

_____

_____

Now let's climb side by side up the jungle gym and answer these questions as we climb:

What do you see ahead of you as you climb?

_____

_____

_____

_____

_____

What enabled you to climb as high as you are?

_____

_____

_____

_____

How does it feel to climb and be in motion?

_____

_____

_____

_____

_____

What did you need to start climbing?

_____

_____

_____

_____

_____

How high can you climb?

_____

_____

_____

_____

_____

For me, reframing the climb is essential to actually being able to climb. Thinking of a jungle gym, there are many ways to go: up, down, right, left, under, over, and all the zigzags along the way. Therefore, the jungle gym also represents resilience, tenacity, and the courage to explore the unknown or to seek a new route or experience. Experiences educate us, they build our confidence, they shape our worldview, and they give us the perspective to see outside of ourselves.

> "Life has a way of pushing, and pulling, and moving you in different directions. You may even fall down. When you get back up, make sure your next move is your best move!"
>
> —Tony Bracken

Sit at the Top, Don't Get Stuck Looking Up from the Bottom

At every turn, I strived to turn fear into faith, kept climbing and navigating the zigzags. I didn't follow one path up the ladder; I embraced every turn, every detour. Find the path that works for you, lean in when it gets hard and the path narrows, and continue to push forward to your goal.

Ultimately, the power to lead is yours on any path; that power is what differentiates employees, intrapreneurs, and entrepreneurs. Be grateful for your own journey and know that it will be different from anyone else's. You have my permission to stay on the path that is right for you.

> "While I am so grateful for all of the stops and starts and wins and challenges I've had in my life, one thing that I think didn't really hit me until I was in my forties is that, wow, this trajectory has been my trajectory, and it's been my journey, and I am grateful for every step of it."
>
> —Nyakio Grieko, founder of Nyakio Beauty, Thirteen Lune, and Relevant: Your Skin Seen

8

Intention of Time: Balancing What's Important

My best friend, my champion, my trust partner, my husband, and my lifer is Pleas Ferguson. We met during our freshman year of college in October 1998 when I was at a party at his college, Wabash. He played basketball, was 6'7", and made my heart burst. We got married in 2008 and in 2014, we had our daughter, Tierra Ferguson, which broadened our range of love and compassion for each other and our family. When I have moments of wanting to sit at the bottom of the jungle gym, I reclaim gratitude for the loves of my life. My priorities start and end with my family.

In 2018, I read a quote that Steve Jobs gave when he was dying from cancer that continues to be present in my mind. It grounds and humbles me when I take myself and work all too seriously, or when I go too long without carving out what is important.

161

Pleas, Kendra, and Tierra, June 2022, Los Angeles

A series of text messages wishing my husband and me a Happy Anniversary from my close friend and business colleague, Farrah Louviere Cerf.

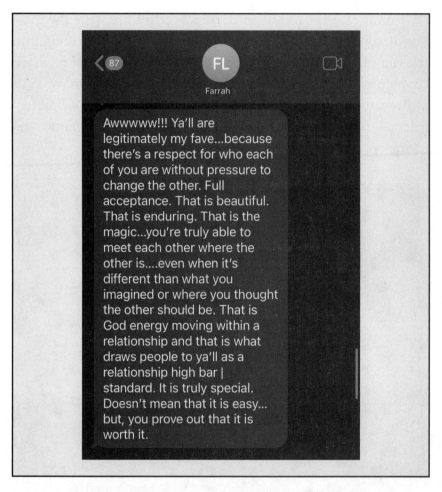

I reached the pinnacle of success in the business world. In some others' eyes, my life is the epitome of success. However, aside from work, I have little joy. In the end, my wealth is only a fact of life that I am accustomed to. At this moment, lying on my bed and recalling my life, I realize that all the recognition and wealth that I took so much pride in have paled and become meaningless in the face of my death. You can employ someone to drive the car for you, make money for you but you cannot have someone bear your sickness for you. Material things lost can be found or replaced. But there is one thing that can never be found when it's lost—Life.

—*Steve Jobs*

Family, friends, and other personal relationships are the most important thing in life. When we are so focused on making it to the top of the jungle gym that we talked about in the previous chapter, we can often lose sight of what's really important to us as humans. And while I believe there is never a day of perfect balance, there is always a chance to rebalance the time and energy you spend on what is important in your life.

Pleas and Kendra's 10-year wedding anniversary, with family and close friends

Each day, we should look at the day before and acknowledge where we can do better for ourselves, for our family, and for our team. We must constantly be resetting the intention and balance of our time. I personally struggle with not being able to go back and change things, but I have learned that we need to let the past go and continue to improve for tomorrow. Don't let things that didn't go perfectly haunt you and stop your forward motion toward greatness.

When I think about forward motion, and betterment across ourselves, our families, and what's important, one of the most powerful leadership stories is from Joni Odum, CEO of Firstline Brands, the first African American–owned hair accessory products company founded in 1986 by Joni's late father, Robert A. Bowser. Joni discusses her journey to becoming the CEO of Firstline, a position she initially never considered for herself, and the magnitude of impact she has been able to drive by carving out what is important to continue and expand her family legacy.

Joni A. Odum, an enthusiastic Texas-bred entrepreneur, leads Firstline Inc., a personal products company based in Houston, Texas. Founded in 1986, Firstline is the first African American–owned hair accessory products company with national distribution in top mass retailers such as Walmart and Target; top drug chains, including Walgreens and CVS; top beauty retailers such as Sally Beauty; and various other U.S.-based and international retailers. Designed for consumers with textured hair, Firstline's core product lines include Evolve®, WavEnforcer®, DriSweat®, Camryn's BFF®, and Sleek®. Joni attributes much of her success to her values, cultural experiences, education, and work ethic. She was most inspired sitting in the boot-camp-style classroom under the tutelage of her late father and founder of Firstline, Robert A. Bowser. With Robert's direction, she spent summers as a child observing his leadership and packaging wrap caps in Firstline's manufacturing facilities to years later leading innovation efforts for the company. Throughout her childhood, Robert purposely cultivated an entrepreneurial spirit and energy in both of his daughters to prepare them for life's opportunities and challenges.

Joni Odum and her father, Robert Bowser

Joni's gregarious nature fosters an appreciation of people and wanting them to do well and feel good about themselves. She is personally responsible for penetrating new markets for Firstline and innovating various new products in the company's portfolio alongside others in the pipeline. Early in her career at Firstline, she quickly became the person in charge of culture-building, developing people, and motivating others to lead. Her core competencies are new product development, developing people, business partnering, and building strategies through an opportunistic, financial lens. Her leadership is vital in Firstline's continued growth and expansion of product lines and placement across the country.

Business of the Beat Excerpt, in Conversation with Joni Odum, CEO, Firstline Brands

Season 2, Episode 41, November 6, 2022

edited for print

Kendra Bracken-Ferguson
Podcast Host

Joni Odum
President & CEO of Firstline

Kendra: I'm so excited to dig in today because you truly are an inspiration and the true definition of generational inheritance that we are striving to create at BrainTrust Founders Studio. And for everyone listening as Joni tells her story, I had the esteemed honor and pleasure of meeting her late father and the founder of Firstline, Robert A.

(continued)

Bowser, and being able to sit in a room with them together witnessing the true legacy that Joni is carrying on today and for generations to come.

Joni: I grew up with the entrepreneurial spirit of my dad, who was building a business from nothing. Both of my parents were focused on my sister and I being successful, but also being loved and nurtured. There was a balance in our day-to-day of both. They wanted us to go along the track in our lives that would lead to our happiness. For as long as I can remember, I never knew a time when my father wasn't in business. By the time I was three, he had established his first company that would later catapult him into this business that we have been in for 36 years.

But that meant that I would kind of have this feeling that there are limitless opportunities in life, because I never did think that there wouldn't be a possibility for me to go into anything that I wanted to go into. And then it also taught me just resilience, because I saw the ups and downs of him in business. And so just growing up in that and then just the strength of that made me want to find something that I was passionate about, that I loved, that I could be happy doing, because that was the environment that I grew up in.

But that also was kind of a pressure that I put on myself because I wanted to be successful with whatever it was, because that's what I saw in my father and my mom, just whatever they were doing by any means necessary. But they wanted to be happy. They wanted to love it and be passionate about it, but they wanted to be successful. And so that meant that I really wanted to do my own thing. So I grew up kind of having a posture of, "Dad, this is a great business that you built, amazing. But I'm going to be over here. I'm going to be over here doing what I feel like I am destined to do." And I feel like he was supportive of that.

He never did put any undue pressure or stress on me to go this direction. And he made very subtle hints along the way without telling me certain things. He did that by telling me things that I was very good at, telling me what my personality and my natural ability seemed to be probably drawn to.

But that just to me, it inspired me wanting to go into business, but for what I wanted to do, what I knew I would be passionate about. And so that's what led me to go into kind of a marketing room, and I loved it as my major. I went to Hampton, and this experience would give me kind of a broad experience of being successful.

But then I was convinced by a professor to shift my major to finance because I was doing really well in my finance class. Finance was so high in demand, and I really did love it as well. Right after graduating, I went into a financial leadership development program at Johnson and Johnson (J&J), which provided an excellent background in finance. Basically, I did rotations throughout J&J to different subsidiaries, just learning different areas of finance. J&J really were preparing future leaders to lead within finance, and so I thought it was great exposure. It's funny because I met my husband at J&J, as well.

On my last rotation, I was the person responsible for managing the brand marketing expenses for all of the advertising efforts of the Tylenol Marketing Group. It was so exciting working closely with the brand, and it showed

(continued)

me my love for marketing. I loved being a part of what was driving the brands and I started to appreciate the marketing side of the business and also having a financial lens along with it.

And that's the day that I decided that I would help my dad. I would bring some of that knowledge back to our family-owned business, and just in any way possible, try to help him in his efforts to scale and to do all the wonderful things that we did years down the road.

I discovered that a lot of the work the marketing team was doing were also things that I could help my dad do.

That was the *aha* moment—that it's great that I'm doing it for these huge, big-box brands, and these brands that are national brands around the world. They're global, and I was able to help make an impact on those. But how much of an impact could it be on this small brand? At the time it [Firstline Brands] was a small brand that hadn't really reached its level of recognition yet. There was so much work to be done, but so much opportunity in that. I just felt like I'm over here making a difference at a $30 billion company. But over here, at our family business, I can make such a bigger impact in what my dad is building, that the magnitude would be far greater, and I could bring what I've learned.

I was trained by state-of-the-art companies that really had some of the best training programs around the world. And so the ability to bring that back just was very rewarding for me. And so I feel like there was a reason that journey happened in that order.

Joni brought her institutional knowledge back to the family business. It is the perfect reflection of finding the space to maintain the importance of balancing love, family, and business intertwined to evoke lifelong happiness. She shares so deeply and passionately about the reward and importance of her decision to come back to the family business and the magnitude of the impact she could make.

When you think about the future of your success, the foundation of all you can and will accomplish, what is most important to you?

_____

_____

_____

_____

_____

Tackling Important Moments Every Day

For me, identifying what is important has two paths that are deeply intertwined. When I think about what is important in life (my family, my faith, my health) and what is important in work (fueling my passion, generating profit, delivering on a promise), claiming, holding, and staying true to these things are essential. My intention of time and balancing that time is essential, as is the connectivity between my personal and professional life.

Time has been a consistent Achilles heel. Although it's difficult to make time for family, time for my husband, time for myself, time for work, and time for calls, understanding and defining time helps. I choose to define time this way as a metric of protecting my time:

Tackle
Important
Moments
Every day

Now for me, the *I* is what throws me off: figuring out each day what is important in the sea of everything that seems important or imperative in that moment.

So I have to drill down my own definition of important. According to Dictionary.com, here are a few ways to explain the word *important*:

Definition of **important**:
   adjective
   of much or great significance or consequence
   mattering much (usually followed by *to*)
   entitled to more than ordinary consideration or notice
   prominent or large
   of considerable influence or authority, as a person or position
   having social position or distinction, as a person or family
   pompous; pretentious

"Just taking the time to honor the gift of time means honor this day. Right now, this is the only day I have. In this moment, right now, this is the only moment we can really say yesterday is gone. Tomorrow is TBD. When you really slow down and honor the pace of life, it allows you to be present for the extraordinary. I think for a lot of people, if you've been fortunate to where your life has not been severely disrupted by these pandemics, you've had an opportunity to reset your pace and to realize and to watch the seasons change. To watch the leaves and to watch that in nature, everything has a pace and you cannot plant anything today and eat fruit tomorrow. In our world with its technology, in some ways, if we don't watch it, we expect life to match, technology to be instant and everything, we have such luxury that we can sometimes cloud our vision.

"The secret to the extraordinary is to stay in the now, to stay present to what I am feeling now. How am I wiggling my toes? Did I stretch today? How am I moving in my body? What am I excited to eat for lunch? That is the secret sauce for me. Your life is right now. What are you going to do now?"

—Charreah Jackson, media strategist and executive coach, Shine Army, and best-selling author, *Boss Bride*

So when I further deconstruct this, I look at importance with an undertone of joy, passion, and happiness.. . . Is there a consequence if I don't do this one thing today? Can I do it tomorrow so that I can do something that brings me more peace or contentment? When I go to bed tonight, can I say I *carved out* time for what is important to me, so that I can say my time was spent **T**ackling **I**mportant **M**oments **E**very day?

Email from Julie

YOU are incredible.

BE PROUD of yourself for all you do.

And I wonder if you could allow SMALLER spaces (of time) to OPEN inward.

EVEN 5 minutes can make a difference! if you BREATHE and TURN off everyone ELSE~!

LITTLE bits of **TIME** stolen back for YOU! to BREATHE

to have SUPPORT!

to have some of what you NEED.

As emailed to me by Julie Flanders on October 12, 2022, in regard to taking time for myself

---

Through my conversation with Joni, my work with Julie, and so many others, the acknowledgment of what is important from claiming joy, defining happiness on your own terms, and loving yourself is a vital ingredient to balancing your time. When we remember our *why* and hold to that *why*, it makes it easier to keep these close.

I invite you to go back to what is important daily. Write it down as a daily affirmation to yourself and keep it close.

9 | Stand in Your Power

Never give up. Just at that moment when you're about to give up is when it happens.
——Tonya Lewis Lee, founder of Movita Organics

Clarity on who you are, what you want out of life, and how you choose to spend your time is the key to success and job satisfaction. As intrapreneurs you must be clear on your boundaries and how much of yourself you are willing to give to someone else's company. Are you being celebrated, are you being rewarded, are you being fulfilled? Are you diminishing your power to give it to someone else? As entrepreneurs, do you have the freedom that being your own boss can provide? Are you leveraging your best gifts to grow your business?

In season 3 of *Business of the Beat*, I had the profound honor of going deep with Tonya Lewis Lee. We agreed that our word for 2023 was em(Power)ment and the notion of standing in your power, specifically as Black women, and the importance of nonnegotiables, collaboration, and giving back to our communities. Tonya credits her partners for enabling her to leverage her gifts to build and grow Movita Organics centered around educating, empowering, and supporting women in their own unique health journeys.

Tonya Lewis Lee is a producer, film director, writer, entrepreneur, and women's health advocate, delivering meaningful content that resonates with marginalized communities for over 20 years. Her work often explores the personal impact of social justice issues, health and wellness. Most recently, Lee co-directed and co-produced the documentary *AFTERSHOCK*, now streaming on Hulu, which examines the Black and Brown maternal mortality crisis in America. The film premiered at the 2022 Sundance Film Festival, winning the Special Jury Award for Impact for Change, and continues to garner rave reviews and noteworthy press. As a film and television writer, producer, and director, her work has spanned family-friendly features like *The Watsons Go to Birmingham* as well as the episodic series *She's Gotta Have It*, streaming on Netflix. She also produced *Monster*, which premiered at the 2018 Sundance Film Festival and is streaming on Netflix. In 2007, Tonya became the spokesperson for the U.S. Department of Health and Human Services Office of Minority Health's infant mortality awareness campaign, A Healthy Baby Begins with You, which ignited her lifelong passion of advocating for better health outcomes for all women in the United States, especially women of color. Through the campaign, Tonya produced the film *Crisis in the Crib: Saving Our Nation's Babies*. This work led Tonya to embark on her journey as an entrepreneur to create Movita Organics, a premium vitamin supplement brand, to continue the conversation with women about accessing healthy outcomes and provide them with a high-quality resource to aid their well-being and overall vitality. An acclaimed author, Tonya has created books, including *Please, Baby, Please*, that have entertained children and young adults throughout her career. Tonya has been featured in notable outlets including ABC's *Nightline*, *CBS Mornings*,

New York Magazine's *The Cut, Essence, Vogue,* and more. She is the mother of two adult children and lives in New York City with her husband, Spike Lee.

Kendra Bracken-Ferguson
Podcast Host

ft. Tonya Lewis Lee
Producer, Director, Writer,
Women's Health Advocate &
Founder of Movita Organics

SEASON THREE

Business of the Beat **Excerpt, in Conversation with Tonya Lewis Lee, founder, Movita Organics**

Season 3, Episode 6, February 12, 2023

edited for print

Kendra: I want to start with what is one word you would use to describe the start of 2023?

(continued)

Tonya: I would say *empowerment*. *Power* is the word I would use for the start of 2023.

Kendra: I love that word. And I think with so many things that are happening in the world, being able to really stand in our own power and understand what that means and define it for ourselves is important. It can be a hard thing to understand.

Tonya: I think so. And I think as Black women, I certainly feel at my age, I am just really beginning to understand my power and to not give it away. To really stand in my power and to use my power in a way that works for me and for those around me, my friends, my family, my community, and really guard that power and wield it really well.

I see expansion and growth on the horizon for Black women in particular. I think if anyone's really paying attention to what's happening out here, the old saying is if you want to get something done, you put a Black woman in the place to get it done. And like, you see that time and time again. Just like the clerk right now in Congress is a Black woman, the head clerk, and there's another Black woman. So there are two Black women right now who are actually running Congress. So I think if anyone is really paying attention to who gets things done in a really great way, I think they will see that Black women time and time again show up who are incredibly skilled, thoughtful, and amazingly functional under so many different types of stress, so many different kinds of obstacles that come in our way.

So I think it's a really exciting time for us as Black women. I think it always has been. I just think that sometimes the industries need to really pay attention and catch up and really understand who we are and how we always show up time and time again.

Kendra: It's also about the support we have as Black women and our allies, a valuable lesson I've learned to help me stand in my power.

Tonya: And I have to tell you, I have great partners in Movita: a guy named Robert Sires and then another guy named John Passmore. I really appreciate them because as a Black woman, often people try to play you. They don't hear you. It's amazing. It's amazing. I'll say something, and it's like, I didn't say it and keep coming back. And Bob, who happens to be a white guy, will say—and he's so great—he's like, What is wrong with them? Didn't they hear what you said? And I'm like, thank you, Bob. Thank you. It's been a while now that we've been working together, and it's really wonderful to have partners in Movita that are solid, that have your back, that see things, and we don't always agree, but we can talk it out and see things.

In a way, it's a game changer. I couldn't do this business if I didn't have them in a way that was really solid and had my back as I have theirs.

Kendra: It's interesting. The first company I started, I had a co-founder. And then when I started BrainTrust in 2015, I didn't have a co-founder, and then in 2022, I brought in a co-founder for the studio and the fund. I'm so happy I did. It's truly someone to have your back, carrying the weight. It is also important when your voice may not be heard . . . back to standing in your power.

Tonya: Exactly. And look, collaboration, I love collaboration. Collaboration is the name of the game. And the best collaboration is like when you're brainstorming and you're talking ideas and you got an idea and someone's like, oh, yeah, and you said that and that made me think this, and

(continued)

you're like, Right. And then you keep building and building on the idea. Like having great brains work it out. It's just so much fun. Nothing is better than that to me.

Kendra: In addition to standing in your power, collaboration, and having great brains to work it out, what is another piece of entrepreneurial advice?

Tonya: I would tell other founders as my best piece of advice to be in it for the long haul and understand that being an entrepreneur is tough. It's highs and lows. And when the highs are high and it feels so good, you know there's going to be a low and you just have to keep working through it. Never give up. I think if there's a saying or this thought that just at that moment when you're about to give up is the moment when it really is going to happen, and yet and still you also do need to know when to cut your losses. Hang in there. Being an entrepreneur is being a problem solver. And so you just need to show up and solve the problem every day.

All leaders must be clear about who they are when taking on the responsibility of leading others. Before you can lead, you must know and stand in your own power to be the most effective and not get off track to reaching your goal. Sometimes it takes a lot of courage to tap into your full potential, but when you undertake the type of self-actualization that we're discussing in this book, you will be able to stand in your power, which in turn will lead to greater success.

"I'm not fearless, but what I am is courageous, and what I also am is clear."

—Charreah Jackson, founder of Shine Army

If we are not crystal-clear about what we need to achieve our goals, it will be hard to meet them. Charreah Jackson, founder and CEO of Shine Army, says, "If we do not define ourselves for ourselves, others will do it for us, often telling us our stories are bad." She encourages women especially to define their own path to add their own unique flair to what society expects of them.

Charreah decided to leave her high-paying, corporate job to pursue a new path of entrepreneurship. She said that it was difficult to make the transition but that her spirit never lied and that she was able to keep all of the lessons learned from her previous positions when she jumped into her new business. Charreah advises setting goals and timelines for ourselves, staying true to ourselves, and trusting our own power and intuition when making big decisions.

When you are able to stand in your power by knowing your value, honoring what you uniquely bring to the table, boldly expressing your goals, and claiming your nonnegotiables, your life truly can be extraordinary on your own terms.

Charreah Jackson is a media strategist and executive coach, founder of Shine Army, a contributing writer for the *New York Times*, and an author. She began her career as an editorial assistant at *Essence* magazine and then was the senior editor for over a decade. Jackson has experience working for fashion and beauty PR firms with clients such as Disney, House of Harlow, and TRESemmé . She is also the author of *Boss Bride*, which I have in my own personal library, the powerful women's playbook for love and success. She is passionate about health and wellness, a previous Wellness Coach for Weight Watchers (WW), and was named by the National Association of Professional Women as "Woman of the Year."

WITH CHARREAH JACKSON
HOSTED BY KENDRA BRACKEN-FERGUSON

Business of the Beat **Excerpt, in Conversation with Charreah Jackson, founder, Shine Army**

Season 1, Episode 9, February 6, 2021

edited for print

Charreah: I am excited to be here. Oh, my gosh, I love you, and I love that you are unlocking your incredible knowledge in your network. I'm buckled up to listen and share.

Kendra: Thank you! Please share everything. This is about both of us coming together, and I just want to start with this. I follow you on IG, and of course I know you in real life, and across both there is consistency, and I am always inspired. It's just contagious how you uplift people. Just kind of fill me in because we met in your *Essence* days and now you have Shine Army and are on the ministry team at Wheat Street Baptist Church.

Charreah: Yes, the ways I serve have expanded, but the mission has stayed the same. I'm simply on the planet to support people to own their story and share their story with the world. And so that's something I'm super-excited about. At my core, I'm a storyteller and a messenger, and one of the most important things we ever do is to honor our own story. That's what I do as a coach. That's what I do as a minister. I'm at one year of being on the ministry team at my childhood church in Atlanta. I'm also on the ministry team at my second church, Home Change Church, which is based out of New Jersey with locations around the world. It's funny because I would love to be like, wow, that's amazing. Even as I'm sitting talking right now, I'm in my office and I have a vision wall, and I have a portrait of my third great-grandparents, who were both born into slavery.

My third great-grandfather founded 14 churches after he started; while he was still in slavery, he used to host church services under what kind of looks like a teepee fortress of branches. He was given land and built a church and went on to create 14 churches. It is in my blood. Part of me honoring my own legacy is part of helping other people realize that we all have a legacy. I met you in the days of

(continued)

being an editor and I am still a journalist, I still am a contributor now for the *New York Times*. It's all about the power of story. For me, what's always been the core thread for me is the power of story and what happens when we own our story, what happens when we pick up the pen and write our own story, which I do with my clients.

Kendra: I mean, there's so much in what you said in terms of legacy, power, and it's so important to come to the table for ourselves and to help write our story. Not even to help, but to drive and to write our story. There's so much power in picking up a pen, we spend so much time attached to technology and always being on our phones. I really believe there's something about journaling and this power of storytelling for yourself to unlock self-actualization that enables you to move forward.

In terms of legacy, we are both around a lot of different people who call themselves legends. You said that you always include your middle initial *K* to honor your great-grandmother, and that you said you were named after her because it's part of your legacy and that you really encourage people to identify and live their legacy.

So what does legacy mean, and why is it so important?

Charreah: First, thank you for sharing. I started doing that the year my grandmother passed away in 2009. I felt like I was missing that connection. What legacy is and why it's important is it honors the fact that we all come to this planet with an inheritance because, to your point, it's not about the world's definition of what a legend is. We all are inside of a legacy, and so we miss out on so much power and fuel for our lives when we don't tap into what legacy we are part of. Yes, it's a part of your family, but it's not just your family. I'm very proud. I'm a Howard University graduate and I was managing editor at our newspaper, which was founded by Zora Neale Hurston in 1924. Over 80 years later, I'm there as an editor because she started something.

One of my coaching programs that's launching next week is called Legend, and it's all about helping people because I realize for me, that's really one of my strengths.

People say, Oh, my gosh, you're so strong. You're fearless. I'm not fearless, but what I am is courageous. And what I also am is clear. When you start to really tap into legacy, it gives you clarity and power because you're like, Oh, wow, I don't have to do everything by myself. Oh, wow, there are people who are part of my community. You get to be a part of the world that you inhabit, and even anywhere you go, you don't feel so alone.

Because we are in a time in society where people, the rates of loneliness are astronomical, and the pandemic has only exacerbated that issue, that people feel isolated and alone. One of the antidotes for that is connection. But also, what legacy am I building? Who's coming behind me? What are my ways to step up and ensure that the work that I'm generating and creating isn't lost when I'm no longer able to run it?

Kendra: It's so powerful. I think that's one of the things, especially in COVID, people talk about being isolated because we've been quarantined, and you can be in a room full of people and still feel isolated, but when you're physically isolated, it really does do something different to you. I think that it's also brought about this sense of immortality.

(continued)

We lost my husband's aunt in the middle of COVID, and death during this time of isolation seems to have just changed the way that we grieve, the way that we show up. It also starts to make you think about legacy. It's exactly what you said: What legacy are you building? In actuality our legacy is so much more than just our family and ourselves.

Charreah: I just love this conversation and I love you for holding space for conversations like this because it is important, because particularly in the days of social media, it's easy to just see the results and the receipts and the high-light reels, to not know what people really feel on the inside. I think any great leader, any great person who's looking to make an impact, is choosing a large dose of fear to come, because even your biggest dreams will scare you, because it is outside of your comfort zone. People think that they can stay right in their comfort zone and have an extraordinary life when it doesn't live there. You literally have to leave the neighborhood of your comfort zone to go get the thing you've never had and live in your power.

Inside of the scariest moment, to your point, is also where so many blessings occur. Part of what allows us to move in spite of the fear is the courage of actually, fear isn't driving this ship. And I love Elizabeth Gilbert. She's got this *Dear Fear* letter where she talks about, I'm about to go on this exciting adventure called Fear.

I think for some when you don't feel afraid, you're playing too small. I say all the time, I'm just not playing small, coach. If you're waiting to feel excited and that you got it to get moving, you will never move. Underneath all of that, to your point, is clarity. When you're clear about who you are, when you're clear about why you are, then the fear does not have so much control. You talk about my journey and I often share it. Before turning 25, I battled cancer. I had been laid off in the recession. I had found out I was the other woman in a new relationship, unbeknownst to me. I say that to say I had to face real life real early.

It made me clear because I didn't have the luxury of pretending that I have forever to live. I didn't have the luxury of pretending that someone else was going to come save me or that I had to look for love outside of myself. And so that's where the clarity comes. It's not that I don't know, I'm throwing stuff at the wall too. I'm hoping it all goes well too. I think for a lot of people, resetting who you are with yourself and resetting ultimately what you're up to will give you access to more power.

Kendra: I remember when I was at Ralph Lauren. I was the first director of digital media and I thought I was going to be there forever. When I wanted to leave to start my first company, Digital Brand Architects, I remember a meeting I had with the chief of staff, who at the time just happened to be the only senior Black woman in a position of power. And she was amazing. She said, "Okay, seems like you have a good business plan, access to the bloggers, and experience. And fundamentally your last name isn't Lauren and if it doesn't work, you can always try something else or you can come back."

Charreah: Wait a minute. Can we just sit in what you just said? Because how many times do we get lost in wearing somebody else's name more proudly than we wear our own name? It took courage to say I trust enough that

(continued)

I don't need the coat. Yes, it's a nice coat that fit for a season. I'm grateful. I learned a lot. I don't need the coat of the Lauren name to validate me because also what happens and part of the clarity, what happens for a lot of people, they're not clear around their validation, where it's coming from. Am I self-validated or do I need that external validation?

For you to have that courage, which leads to this moment, which leads to so many extraordinary things you've generated, I just want to honor that because I think it is harder to take off a really nice coat. That was a really nice coat for a season. I think it's important to acknowledge and we live in a culture that says that somebody else's validated name is better than validating your own name. And what you did was validate. You are enough. I have what it takes to build for what you haven't even seen yet because you were building something people hadn't seen yet. So I'm just like, powerful. I think it's important because people often ask, Well, how did you do it?

When it's validated, they're like, Well, I want to do it. Before that, it's like you have to jump before you have the evidence. You have to have enough inside to trust that you've got it, that I'm willing to let go of something that the world tells me is the mountaintop.

Sometimes we think we're too much. We start to police, How much am I too much? Are they going to be able to receive me? It's also not only am I enough, I'm also not too much. There might be people who can't handle the fullness of me that's on them. Put your sunglasses on. It's not on me to try to minimize myself for the comfort of others. Find your legacy and stand in your power.

Define, Claim, and Own Your Power

Whether you are an intrapreneur or entrepreneur, you need to believe in your value, your importance, and your worth, meaning you need to stand in your power. Both types of leaders are needed to fuel our economy and our society. One path is not more important than the other.

I am grateful that I was an intrapreneur before I was an entrepreneur. I believe there is value from taking time to learn, listen, and watch how business works. I would not have been as successful as an entrepreneur if I had started that journey right out of college. I needed time to develop, sit in boardrooms, and learn how to navigate the corporate landscape. I also needed to navigate my ego to learn about meekness as a characteristic of power and establish my own self-actualization process to instill confidence in myself to lead people as a decision-maker.

Those are the tenets of understanding how to lean in and stand in your power but first I had to unlock my own innate powers and build on those through time spent and experience gained. I needed to establish contacts and build a network. Both of my companies were built through my pillar of community, because my clients were from past relationships that I developed throughout my career. There is something special about being part of a company, learning about culture, about teams connecting to get the job done, and having a front row seat at the dynamics that make companies successful.

After Fleishman, I said I never wanted to do time entry, which is a process where you have to record how you spent your time every day. Every 30-minute interval had to be recorded with a description to bill back to clients or track your utilization, the amount of billable time an employer can pull out of the total available working time for their employees. I made it my mission to not incorporate it into my own company, but after some time of overservicing clients, overutilizing and underutilizing appropriate team members, we eventually had to incorporate time entry into our work flow process.

At that moment, I finally understood why Fleishman made it a priority to track our time. Had I not had the experience, I would never have known how to properly manage my team's time against clients and how to charge for their time. The devil is in the details, and sometimes those minor nuisances can lead to a shift in profitability. I encourage the next group of entrepreneurs to take time to listen, learn, and be mentored. It's not all about how much money you have in the bank to start your venture but about creating a sustainable company that is rooted in experience and knowledge.

After I bought BrainTrust back from CAA-GBG, I had several offers on the table from people/companies to buy it, and I told myself I needed 30 days before I made a decision. Two times in the first two weeks, I almost sold my company again or did a joint venture. It was a rare moment of not feeling like I was enough or that I needed another company to validate me.

Let's face it, I was scared and had to get out of my own head to turn my fear into faith. I preach it all the time but yet I still stood in front of my own fear, scared to tell anyone I was terrified, and so I leaned in to these offers, thought about them, and tried to figure out what was wrong with me that I didn't feel grateful enough for those offers to take them. I needed to hold on to my 30 days and amplify my faith.

In church, Bishop Ulmer said, "The faith that got you here is not the faith that will move you forward. You have to increase and grow your faith to make it the next step of the journey." He was right; with fear turned greater faith, more of the "angels" or right people around me, and an awakening in myself that I had not been able to hold and own before. I came face-to-face with defining, claiming, and owning my power. It's not that others wanted to dim my light; they wanted to take it for themselves. For the first time, I understood the mentality of a taker in business. This time, I stood in my power, held my ground for 30 days, and stayed on my path back to entrepreneurialism.

I Choose Me Every Day

I tried so long to be what everyone else wanted and the thing that draws everybody to me is just being myself.

—Junior Mintt, founder of Junior Mintty Makeup

Understanding your value and leaning into the right opportunities and community that supports you was further reflected in my conversation with Junior Mintt, a drag artist, business owner, and motivational speaker based in Brooklyn. She's the creator and producer of *In Living Color*, a drag variety show, and a co-host of the Brooklyn Liberation March. Junior has been featured in *Vogue*, *The Cut*, *ID*, and *Gay Letter* for the work she does not only on stage, but also in the community. She is also the creator of Mintty Makeup, one of the first Black trans makeup lines. Mintty Makeup has been featured in *BuzzFeed*, *Paper Magazine*, *Beauty Matter*, and *Vogue Beauty*.

Business of the Beat Excerpt, in Conversation with Junior Mintt

Season 2, Episode 25, July 17, 2022

edited for print

Kendra Bracken-Ferguson
Podcast Host

Junior Mintt
Founder, Mintty Makeup

LISTEN TO THIS EPISODE ON Apple Podcasts Spotify

Junior Mintt: Thank you for having me. I am just so thankful to get to be in a space with another Black creative individual who's running a business and at the same time not giving up a piece of themselves to do it. I'm like sitting in a space where I'm just grateful because when you look around and see great people, that's how you know you're doing something right because you're with great people.

Kendra: The energy and the connectedness and the support that you radiate is just phenomenal. Of course, it's the eye shadow as well. Let's be real. I can't look at you and not feel good, but I'm excited. I want to read this quote to start because I think it actually fills in with what you said. You said when you were thinking about starting your business and you were talking to one of your friends, he reminded you that there's nothing that you can't do. And that's exactly what he said: "Just start it, why not?"

It resonated with me because I have lived by the mantra *Carpe Diem* my entire life. When I read that, I reached out immediately because I was like, anyone who says, "Just start it, why not?" and does it is my people. So take us back. Tell us who you are, how you became this amazing soul.

Junior Mintt: It all led to when I moved to New York after graduation, because I always like to say, I moved to New York to find Paris is burning, but I found, like, a lukewarm Berlin. It was one of those things where I came here, and I was expecting to see community because I finally understood myself as a queer Black trans woman. But I was never was able to find it because even in New York City, we were being pushed to the margins and not given any type of support or come-up that we deserve. And so I started creating my own spaces. And for over two and a half years, my show, *Living Color*, was the only show in New York produced by a Black trans woman. And we just celebrated our third anniversary.

And it's so funny to me because I remember the first show we did; one of my really good friends came, and we were in a car ride going back home, and they just went, do

(continued)

you know that this is church? Like, do you know that this is queer church? Because it was all about everybody getting to come as who they are. I'm so thankful for the show because I've learned how to stand up for myself and my community in ways that I never could have expected.

And then it was deep into the middle of the quarantine. And my friend asked me what I wanted to do with my career when my body physically couldn't do it [the show] anymore. Because an amazing influencer on Instagram said, It's not a matter of if you become disabled; it's a matter of when. And it was that phrase that always went around in my head. It's like, okay, well, my body physically can't be on stage all the time. What else do I want to do? And that's when it clicked for me. That's when it all clicked because I was like, definitely makeup. Because makeup is the thing that made me realize that I was trans because I would feel so amazing when putting on makeup and then taking it off I'd be emotional and want to cry because I realized the only time I allowed myself to see myself as a woman was when I had makeup on while doing drag.

And I realized that the same power I felt with all the makeup on is a feeling I could have even when I take the makeup off. And when I thought about it, I was like, oh, yeah, I would love to do makeup, but how's that ever going to happen? And they said that to me. They were like, What do you think that you can't accomplish, Junior? Do you not have this amazing show that has survived throughout the pandemic and done all these things? I have housing security. I know where my next meal is coming from. All through my own hard work, I'm the primary caregiver for my mother. And all of which came through my art and being myself. And through [my friend] talking to me about it, I was like, I can do this. I can do this. And in less than a year, we made this deal with Thirteen Lune and JCPenney Beauty. And it blows my mind at the fact that anything I set my mind to, I can accomplish. I'm just so thankful that I have a community around me that reminds me every day that whatever it is that I want to accomplish, I can do it.

Kendra: I am just blown away by you. Your story is so rich, and there's this humility about it that is really about how am I going to be my best self and how do I show up and stand in my power every day? And so many people are repressed, and they can't figure out how to get to the other side. You are also big on kindness and empathy. Two things that, quite frankly, Black and Brown people are really given less of; in so many spaces, we're not treated kindly and we're not treated with empathy. How have those traits helped you navigate and move through this world in a softer way?

Junior Mintt: I am so thankful for my mom. She is my biggest cheerleader, my biggest fan. She was born in 1958, and at a very young age, people tried to take her softness from her. She was one of the first kids who was a part of busing Black kids into white schools and was picked on severely. However, she just refused to have her softness taken away.

It was one of those things that I'm so thankful for, because my softness is the thing that I've realized is my faith and grace in my life. Because for me, it is the thing that tells me to listen to myself. It's the thing that reminds me that if somebody gives you toxic or negative energy, I love you and me enough to not be in this situation. I'm going to

(continued)

love myself enough to give myself space from this thing that I can tell is not good enough for me. It's all about understanding that there is no malice in anything. There's only love. I love you enough to know that obviously, we do not get along, so let me love you enough to let you go.

It is all about maintaining your softness in it all because the world is built up in order to make you hard. That's what the system is built to do. Because when you're hard, that's when you feel like there's a product that you need. There's something that you need to fill your life, when really the only thing you need to survive in this world is you and yourself. Everything else naturally comes with it. Because when you're yourself I know that if I wasn't able to pay my rent today, I have multiple people who would either, one, give me the money, or two, be like, I will set up a GoFundMe for you right now. We will get through all of this together.

That softness builds the community without you even having to try, because softness makes people feel seen. When you choose to be vulnerable around somebody, even when you don't know them, that's an act of strength. That's an act of saying, I know myself well enough to know that I fit into any situation just by being myself, and I don't have to have a hard experience in order to hold my boundaries. And boundaries don't necessarily meet aggression. Boundaries are another form of love. I love you enough to tell you what you won't do to me.

Kendra: I love you enough to tell you what you will not do to me. That is the purest form of self-love. I think that so many people have to understand that. I remember my mom would say, Don't put yourself in a situation where people take you out of your character. There's been these moments when we talk about our moms and their influence and the impact, and it's just fascinating because I found myself in business situations where I was acting out of character in order to belong in the environment of which I thought I needed to be in to achieve success as an entrepreneur. When you get in those places, then you have to remove yourself and realize that's not meant for me because that's not how I want to show up and move in the world and having the self-actualization and ability to acknowledge that.

Junior Mintt: I don't want to be in any space where I can't bring my full self. As well, when bringing my full self, being supported in that and that means that if I tell you that somebody says something transphobic, not questioning me, believing me the first time when I say that someone is making someone uncomfortable, it shouldn't be a question. It's about understanding that people are meant to be supported. Especially in the moments where I could look at you and see that when you step out the door, you made a choice. Because walking out the door as a Black trans woman every single day, I could easily stay in my bed. I can easily put on something that will just allow me to be seen as whatever and not have to be seen walking out the house with this face on. Wearing my dresses and my earrings is a choice.

I choose me every day I wake up, and I could choose to be anybody else. I could choose to say, "Okay, there's going to be people on the street who's going to say something, so let me not wear this." And I choose it. It's so interesting because every time when I do it, if I walk out the door

(continued)

feeling an ounce of insecurity in any way, there always is a Black woman on the street who gives me some type of compliment. I've realized that even in your most insecure, if you're being yourself, you're going to find your community, and your community is going to find a way to uplift you.

Junior talks extensively about choosing herself, showing up for herself, and being her true self. When you stand in your power, you are declaring that you choose yourself every day. You are identifying what you will allow, how you will allow yourself to be treated, and the impact being your true self will have on those around you.

Power doesn't have to be a harsh term defined by aggression or towering over someone else. Standing in your power is understanding who you are and that you are the lead star in your own movie, your own life, your own experience. When you realize and actualize your own power, you can significantly change the outcome of any situation. In the words of Junior Mintt, "It's truly just being able to use all the tools in your toolbox in order to discover your own self first."

At the end of each day, as I stand in my power and in gratitude for all I have accomplished that day, I say to myself, "I am a powerful being. Today, I stand in my power. I am a **P**urveyor **O**f **W**isdom, **E**very day **R**eclaiming myself."

Purveyor
Of
Wisdom
Every day
Reclaiming myself

Feel free to repeat my daily mantra, or you can define POWER on your own terms:

P _____

O _____

W _____

E _____

R _____

10 | Greater Than You Can Imagine

Then Adonai answered me and said: "Write down the vision, make it plain on the tablets, so that the reader may run with it. For the vision is yet for an appointed time. It hastens to the end and will not fail. If it should be slow in coming, wait for it, For it will surely come—it will not delay."
—Habakkuk 2:23 TLV bible.com/bible/314/hab.2.2-3.TLV

Entrepreneurs must be willing to risk everything in order to move forward. So what if this entrepreneur journey is greater than you can ever imagine? What happens if it works? My initial goal for BrainTrust Founders Studio was to raise $2.5 million. I felt comfortable because I had done it before. I wasn't envisioning the greater version of my vision that would later manifest itself.

I have always been a glass-half-full person, and I always start with believing in the greatest outcome. I trust people quickly and expect everyone to do the right thing. While it doesn't always work out that way and I have experienced setbacks from trusting too fast, leaning in too hard, and believing that certain people were out for my good when really they never had the intention of doing the right thing, I will always choose positivity, faith in the best outcome, and that things can and will be greater than you can imagine.

What I have learned is that we can single-handedly restrict and constrain our dreams. The mind is a powerful tool, and we can suppress the expansion of our ideas when we get in our own way. For me, this is where faith comes into play. When I look back at my Culture Index or the risks I have taken, I am fundamentally wired to be a brand architect, an entrepreneur, a visionary.

Take one moment and write the biggest dream you have for your career.

_____

_____

_____

_____

_____

Now look at what you wrote and see if you can dream even bigger. How big can you expand your vision?

_____

_____

_____

_____

_____

Move Out of Your Own Way

I was sitting at dinner with Lisa Stone and our friend Ndidi Oteh, senior managing director of retail strategy and consulting lead (West region) at Accenture, talking about creating an investment vehicle to support the founders in BrainTrust Founders Studio.

As I said, my initial goal was raising $2.5 million to invest in founders. In my mind, that was my limit and a stretch goal, as I didn't have a degree in finance, I wasn't a Goldman Sachs alum, and I didn't have experience in venture capital. I wasn't an investor (yet).

But as we started to talk, Ndidi shook her head and said, "I just don't understand why so small . . . it needs to be bigger."

I started sweating, I felt uncomfortable, and I immediately excused myself to go to the bathroom. After deep breaths and a prayer, I came back collected and ready to receive her feedback. Without hesitation, we agreed to adding multiple zeroes to BrainTrust Fund I.

When I got home, my daily prayer text came through. God gives you nuggets when you are on the right path.

Today's Prayer: Genesis 43
Father, if my vision is too small, change it so it matches Yours.

And just like that, I pushed my vision to be far greater than I ever imagined.

22 Years of Experience and Beyond

I didn't get there by wishing for it or hoping for it, but
by working for it.
                                                    —Estée Lauder

In season 3 of *Business of the Beat*, I had the opportunity to sit face-to-face with Monaè Everett in person at Blushington's flagship lounge in New York City. This visit was very special because Blushington was one of my first clients when I launched BrainTrust in 2015, and several years later I was invited to join the advisory board. At the time of our conversation, it was just announced that Monaè was joining Blushington as their new global artistic director.

As we sat talking, a recurring theme arose that throughout Monaè's career, her growth and expansion were far greater than she had ever imagined.

Monaè Everett is a celebrity hair stylist and hair visionary that has worked with celebrities including Tia Mowry, Yara Shahidi, Taraji P. Henson, Serena Williams, Danai Gurira, Emily Tosta, and Nickelodeon starlets Lizzy Greene and Sofia Wylie. As a staunch advocate of diversity and inclusion, last year Monaè founded the Texture Style Awards, a new beauty competition celebrating the beauty of hair and honoring the

AMERICAN SALON   Education   Hair   Barbering   Nails   Skin   Products   Business

HAIR

Monaè Everett Joins Blushington As Artistic Director

By American Salon Staff • Sep 7, 2022 12:54pm

(American Salon) (Monaè Everett) (texture) (blowout)

(@monaeartistry)

Image from *American Salon*, "Monaè Everett Joins Blushington as Artistic Director," September 7, 2022

artists who have mastered styling techniques for all hair textures. An author and public speaker with over 22 years of experience, you can find Monaè's work in media ranging from *Harper's BAZAAR* to *O, The Oprah Magazine* and *ESSENCE* to *Hair's How*. Driven by her love to educate, in 2016 Monaè launched "The Monaè Life" online academy specifically for hairstylists, teaching how to style for editorials, celebrities, and all hair textures.

Business of the Beat Excerpt, in Conversation with Monaè Everett

Season 3, Episode 1, January 8, 2023

edited for print

Kendra Bracken-Ferguson
Podcast Host

ft. Monaè Everett
Celebrity Hairstylist
Founder of The Texture Style Awards

SEASON THREE

Kendra: You've added a new role to your title, let's start there.

Monaè: Yes, I am the new global artistic director at Blushington for hair styling. Working with Blushington has been a dream come true. You may know them for their makeup work, but I'm working with them to make sure that they're very diverse and can style any client that comes in through all four hair textures: straight hair, wavy hair, curly hair, and, of course, coily hair.

Kendra: Blushington was literally one of my first clients when I launched BrainTrust agency seven years ago. I'm now on the board and worked with the founders and Natasha Cornstein, the CEO, for several years in multiple capacities.

Monaè: We want to make sure everyone can come in and feel good and look better when they leave.

Kendra: It's such a testament to the era we live in. You have to be able to service the needs of the majority of the consumers. The space of hair textures, styles, and care is so much more expansive than what it was before.

Monaè: It's no longer acceptable to say, I only style one form of hair texture or people who have hair texture like me. Whether your salon focuses on people with straight, wavy, curly or coily hair, now, if you're a general salon, you need to be able to service anyone that comes in. You need to make them feel happy that you are servicing them. You need to make sure that your stylists are confident enough to style whomever comes in and that the client feels really good when they leave, because they look amazing.

Kendra: You have had a career spanning over 22 years; let's talk about this notion of evolution, not just the salon but you as an artist and professional.

Monaè: Well, I started in high school. I was very opinionated whenever I saw celebrities walking on the red carpet at award shows. I would voice my opinion, and people would say, If you can't do any better, you shouldn't say anything. I was like, I think I can do better. I think with a little bit of training, I can make these women look even better. So my thought was, okay, I'll go into cosmetology,

(continued)

and it'll be great. It will allow me to pay for my schooling, my college. And it did. And I didn't expect to stay in the industry, but I found out how vast it is. So I came home, handed my mom my degrees, and went out into the business side of the hair industry. So I worked in salons. I did a lot of different things, but I would always style the hair at photo shoots and for runway shows. I started working with brands and educating them on the industry and hair. And I found out that this beauty industry is just full of so many different options.

Kendra: Well, and that also is the connectivity with the business side. Because you said, I know I can do this better. I'm going to study to do this better. Now I'm doing it better. And then there's the business piece, because if it were just the client, that would be one thing. But the business piece comes in, and I don't think people understand that to be an effective hairstylist for over two decades without the business piece, you're not actually growing your business of hairstyling.

Monaè: I was surprised to learn that any good businessperson works in the business about 30% of the time and on the business about 70% of the time. I said, What do you mean? I thought I could be really great at hairstyling. I didn't know I had to send the invoice, do the marketing, the directing, run the business and the admin. I didn't know I had to do all of that.

Kendra: Well, and when you think about the craft of it, you could just do the craft, but then you wouldn't be Monaè Everett, you wouldn't have all of these business extensions.

Monaè: Absolutely. And now I teach a lot of artists. And I say, There's a woman in church every Sunday who sounds just as good, if not better than Beyoncé. But the world doesn't know her name. We know Beyoncé because she's doing something else. She's doing something more to make herself stand out.

Kendra: So many founders I talk to say Okay, I have this great idea, I'm going to put it in the world and I could automatically be a unicorn, or I should be in every retailer. Yes, there are some people who can go in and within two years do this, and that's fantastic but also not the norm for many new businesses. We know that less than 2% of women-started businesses actually make it to their first $1 million in revenue. But there is a sustainability factor that seems to get lost in this urgency and impatient nature of I want it now. Or to your point of Beyoncé, I don't want to do the extra work because I shouldn't have to.

Monaè: Yeah, I say, Well, you know, Beyoncé wasn't doing any extracurriculars and Beyoncé was traveling her whole childhood, and Beyoncé and her family took in Kelly and oh, you don't want to do all that, but you want her career. Okay, let me know how that works out.

Kendra: Meanwhile, when we think about things being greater than we could imagine, look at you. You did the work, you had the marketing piece, you started going beyond behind the chair and truly understanding the business, and then in 2016, you launched *Monaè Life*. What was the transition and why then did you decide to move into that?

(continued)

Monaè: So I launched the Monaè Life Academy because so many people would say, they would DM me and message me on Facebook and say, Hey, I would love to have the career you had. And I misunderstood them to say that they wanted to learn how to style hair. So I opened the Monaè Life Academy, and it was a lot of virtual styling and teaching them techniques, and they were like, Oh, no, big boss, we want to know how you got there. We want the business. We want you to teach us how to get celebrity clients. We want you to teach us how to work at Fashion Week. We want you to teach us how to not get played, how to get that paperwork in. And I was very reluctant, but then I realized, I wish someone would have taught me.

I wish that education was there. I didn't know any working artist that was willing to teach newer artists how to come in. And now I have probably over 400 students enrolled. I have sold over 1,000 books. I have given people probably over 100 jobs, even some of them working with brands as educators. Because many times when we go into cosmetology, we are not taught about this business. It is very much a bare-bones knowledge and understanding of how to move forth in the industry with the expectation that you will continue to excel on your own and take your own courses.

So my intention is to help people not only get the opportunities, but know what to do once they get those opportunities. You can do better. You will do better. I'll help you do better.

Monaè continued to push herself to learn more, to expand her vision, and to help others when they asked. She held her truth and her mission in place while also exploring places that weren't familiar or were unknown. She made it her job to do better and to help others do better. She saw the potential in herself and others through her teaching, her books, her award show, and her talents to create a future that was far greater than she had ever imagined.

> KEEP your values in the right place
> and HOLD your TRUTH
> NO ONE can break you then
> but you CAN STILL bend and flow
> and find your own DANCE in the winds and storms
> so that even when it seems like a hurricane
> you are just MOVING your arms
> and LAUGHING
> at the EXTRA ENERGY that moves around you
> HAVE FUN Kendra
> YOU HAVE what you need
> to have what you want
> WHAT YOU WANT IS ALREADY RIGHT HERE
> it's a TREASURE hunt!
> it's RIGHT there
> you just have to "see" it
> EYES of faith
> SEE
> —Julie Flanders, as shared December 12, 2022

People Who See You, *Seeeee* You

I met Mioshi Hill through our mutual hairstylist and friend, Darico Jackson. I had just moved to Los Angeles, and we met for the first time at Mioshi's baby shower, while I was also pregnant with Tierra. From that moment on, almost a decade ago, our families have been best friends. We stayed in each other's bubble as a source of comfort and support during Covid and continue to be a source of friendship, encouragement, and love.

Kendra and Mioshi, Los Angeles, January, 2018

When your closest friends see your potential and know that your vision will be greater than you ever imagined, it's a beautiful thing and the most special gift. Our real friends see us at all of our truest moments, when we are vulnerable, tired, and on edge. Real friends will tell you like it is and pull you back when you need it. They provide that voice of reason that is different from a spouse or parent. We confide in them and when they express their love and support you know you are living your purpose.

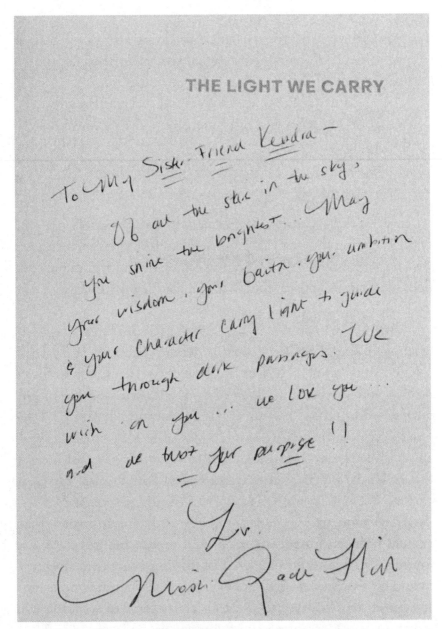

As written to me by Mioshi Hill, December 25, 2022

"Sometimes, you get so settled in doing the thing that you forget to stop and realize what you've done so far, and hearing it, you think, "Oh, God is amazing."
—Jordan E. Cooper, Hollywood star and Broadway sensation, on receiving the Emerging Creatives Award at the inaugural African American Film Critics Associations (AAFCA) Salute to Broadway Awards

In everything you do, no matter what path you are on, start with imagining the best that can happen. Hold that feeling as you navigate your way through. Dream as big as you can without restrictions, without boundaries, and without fear that it won't work out.

Who knew that when we launched BrainTrust Founders Studio in October 2021 that it would become the largest membership-based platform dedicated to Black founders of beauty and wellness companies and encompass each of my pillars—community, mentorship, education, and capital? I set out to create a space for founders with the idea of not leaving any founder behind. I just wanted to be of service and I knew that it was far bigger than me and what I could do on my own.

The vision has expanded globally and grown greater than I could have imagined. It started with emails and calls to a few founders with the ultimate goal of driving economic advancement and pathways to success. We now have a studio and a venture fund, all dedicated to creating ecosystems of winning and investing in underrepresented founders.

I invite you to think back to your own pillars that you wrote down in the Preface and think about the greatness and magnitude that they each unlock. Consider how those pillars can expand into something greater than you ever imagined.

11 | Character, Allyship, and Finding Your People

My mother, Teresa, continues to play a significant role in my life. As her mother, my grandmother, Mary Talley, would say to her and she continues to say to me, "Love the Lord, do what is right, and do your best." Her warmth and constant nurturing was ever-present when I was growing up. She is also quite practical and "real" that things in life will not always be fair, that people will not always treat you right, but that at the end of the day it is our own character, faith, integrity, and how we treat people that will guide us down the right path to live a blessed life. These are all lessons that I will continue to share with my own daughter as she navigates her journey in life.

Four generations: Teresa Bledsoe, Kendra Bracken-Ferguson, Tierra Ferguson, and Mary Talley

This lesson in integrity has been the foundation for me to build community, support others, and be of service. I am very blessed that my mother has been by my side cheering, celebrating, and encouraging me my entire life. She listens to all of my ideas, woes, joys, and ramblings.

We have been through so much, and at every turn my mother has shown tremendous strength and resilience no matter the situation we were in. When I think about these values from childhood, I equate them to character. At the core of my character, I am deeply compelled to do what is right.

Character is an interesting word. What does it actually mean? According to PsychCentral, character represents your ethical, moral, and social attitudes and beliefs. To me it simply means doing what is right even when no one is looking, treating

Photo: Teresa and Kendra, Abilene, Texas, in the family kitchen, 1985

people as you want to be treated, and doing what you say and keeping your word. Words I use to describe my character are integrity, ambition, loyalty, trustworthy.

These traits all must be practiced every day. After all, we are human, we get tired, and we get overcommitted, and that is where our character is challenged in every circumstance. But we should communicate with honesty and transparency. There have been moments when I have committed to something, for example, a meeting, a friend's birthday, or an event that I then have to miss. More times than not, I am shown grace and receive forgiveness based on my ability to take responsibility and say that I was simply overzealous, overambitious, and overly excited. If you live with integrity, you aren't questioned as having malintent when things don't go to plan or your schedule changes. Be truthful in your intent, committed to your word, and steadfast in maintaining your character.

Translating character across my personal beliefs to my work beliefs provides the connective tissue that enables me to stay morally grounded. Throughout my career I have found that our true character comes out in moments of intense stress, turmoil, and difficult conversations. You immediately see people for who they are when they are faced with adversity.

What I learned my first time around as an entrepreneur and doing my first capital raise (that ultimately positioned me in the esteemed group of 100 Black women to raise more than $1 million) was to only seek partners who had the same definition of character, meaning trust, integrity, kindness, and fundamentally doing what is right. Those early encounters taught me how I wanted to lead and the importance of keeping my word. No matter how dire a situation seems, no matter what is happening in business (or your personal life), you should stay true to who you are. It was those encounters that led me to include *trust* in my company name and when it came time to seek a new business partner, I led the search with character.

How do you define character?

_____

_____

_____

_____

_____

What would others say about your character?

_____

_____

_____

_____

What three words describe your character?

_____

_____

_____

_____

The Story of Lisa Stone: Character Meets Allyship

What is the meaning of allyship beyond just treating people right and doing the right, humane thing?

According to Darr Jenkins, a corporate responsibility specialist in inclusion and equity based in the Washington, DC, area, allyship is "an active, consistent, and arduous practice of unlearning and re-evaluation, in which a person in a position of privilege and power seeks to operate in solidarity with a marginalized group." It's an opportunity for personal growth and community development, as everyone has the capacity to be an ally.

As I sat thinking about my place in the industry and how I could do what was right in the wake of George Floyd's murder, the protests in the summer of 2020, and the Black Lives Matter movement, I knew I wanted to create a platform to support Black founders centered around my own pillars of success—community, mentorship, education, and capital.

> "The future belongs to those who can ask for what they want, and advocate for inclusivity."
> —Constance White, award-winning journalist, content creator, editor, and arbiter of culture and style, and past guest on *Business of the Beat* Season 1, Episode 6, January 16, 2021

In the words of Constance, I asked God for what I wanted—the ability and vehicle to support and invest in Black founders—and that blessing came in the form of my co-founder, chief investment officer, and biggest ally, Lisa Stone. Ask and you shall receive.. . . We started with asking each other the tough questions about being partners (how would we be perceived? why was this mission important?, etc.) and being firmly grounded in acknowledging the values and characteristics that are unbreakable in our approach to life and business: integrity, trust, and honesty were at the top of each of our lists.

Kendra and Lisa, Los Angeles, February 2023

Lisa Stone, co-founder, chief investment officer, and general partner of BrainTrust Founders Studio and BrainTrust Fund, is a Silicon Valley builder with multiple exits turned investor. Lisa has raised more than $100 million in venture investment for companies she founded or helped lead, and built five customer movements (25–127 million unique visitors each month) from lifestyle to enterprise, using pricing, programs, and platforms she designed. As an investor, Lisa to date has helped raise more than $125 million from limited partners, including family offices and institutional investors. As a creator economy pioneer, Lisa designed and built scale customer movements and communities (25–127 million monthly uniques) on topics from lifestyle to enterprise (BlogHer, Ellevest, Law.com, Women.com, Hearst, *Fortune* 100 brands, various startups). "Firsts" include: co-founding and leading the first startup to pay more than $50 million to 6,000-plus women bloggers, creating the first blog network publishing model (Law.com), producing a technology-focused women's conference series where consistently more than 30% of speakers were women of color, authoring the first online community guidelines banning hate and harassment, moderating the first town hall by a sitting U.S. president on equal pay for women, and the first Internet journalist awarded a Nieman Fellowship by Harvard University.

I originally met Lisa Stone in the mid-2000s, when she was the CEO of BlogHer, an American media company that she started in 2005 with Elisa Camahort Page and Jory des Jardins. BlogHer was one of my favorite blogging conferences; I remember begging my boss to attend the very first one, and I have attended pretty much every year since.

I met so many fascinating people at BlogHer and eventually became a regular speaker at the conference. In 2021, we announced the launch of BrainTrust Founders Studio during the BlogHer Biz conference in New York. It was our first big announcement for the studio, and I curated a panel with Lisa Price, founder of Carol's Daughter, Ron Robinson, founder of BeautyStat, Dametria Mustin Kinsley, global marketing vice president of Cantu Beauty, and Leyonna Barbar, managing director, technology & disruptive commerce–middle market banking at J.P. Morgan.

B2B+B: Business to Business While Brown Panel, October 21, 2021 New York. Photo provided courtesy of BlogHer. From left Leyonna Barber, Ron Robinson, Dametria Mustin, Lisa Price and Kendra Bracken-Ferguson

Our panel, B2B+B: Business to Business while Brown, explored allyship, the benefits and advantages of differentiated voices, cultural perspectives, and lived experiences across a diverse group of executives and founders and the character traits of what makes a good leader. It was another full-circle moment for me—being at BlogHer onstage with fellow visionaries, founders, and leaders who are all at the top of their fields championing diverse conversations.

Although Lisa had sold and exited BlogHer years earlier, we continued to stay in touch around our shared history of building online media and personalities, the creator economy, and, as we like to say, our love for predictive analytics.

As you know from reading this far into my story, I'm a huge believer in divine timing. Something that has been a guiding light for me my entire career even when I think I may have missed something or a meeting took months to schedule or even in those moments when I may not want to go to the event or attend a meeting—when it finally happens, something magical always happens. Oftentimes after I meet someone, I'm like, "Wow, if I had met you just a week earlier it wouldn't have resonated or been as impactful as it is today." Things always happen in the divine time that they were supposed to.

Funny enough, a friend who Lisa had actually introduced me to about five years prior was having a birthday party in Cabo and invited me to attend. I told Pleas we had to go as I knew something divine would come from the trip. I didn't know what, but it was my heart for God that led us on the journey. Sure enough, the first person we saw at the party was Lisa Stone. We were absolutely "woo girls"—hugging and screaming to see each other, as we had not seen each other in years. It was a divine encounter and one that would forever change my career trajectory and journey.

Little did I know in that moment that we would make history by building BrainTrust Founders Studio and start raising our BrainTrust Fund less than a year after me actualizing my vision to create an ecosystem for Black founders.

Diverse Teams Perform Better

I launched BrainTrust Founders Studio in October 2021 and reconnected with Lisa in January 2022. We proceeded to spend the first few months of 2022 brainstorming, researching, and coming together to create an investment vehicle that would encompass and support our vision.

In March 2022, Lisa and I started raising our first BrainTrust Fund I. One person can't be it all or do it all; we agreed to stand on each other's shoulders and make a way for those around us to grow and thrive.

On May 26, 2022, *Forbes* published an article, "Diversity: The Holy Grail of Venture Capital," which stated that teams that are diverse by gender and ethnicity generate 30% higher MOIC (multiples on invested capital) compared to homogeneous teams. Companies with at least one female or one ethnically diverse founder generate over 60%+ in business value. As evident in our partnership, not only is allyship the right thing to do, it's the smart business thing to do.

According to *Harvard Business Review*,

> 65 percent of venture capital firms have no female partners, and 81 percent have no Black investors at any level. *Less than 3 percent of professionals* in venture capital are Black or Latinx; a *2016 study by Deloitte and the National Venture Capital Association* found that just 3 percent of investment professionals overall are Black. • Despite being world class entrepreneurs, and 7% of the U.S. population, Black Women only receive 1.2% of overall venture dollars invested in the U.S.

You never know what success will look like until you allow yourself to be open to new partnerships, pathways, and opportunities that you may not have been looking for or have imagined. I know that God has blessed me with strong moral character, a powerful light, an aurora of greatness, and a conviction that I will succeed. I don't believe there are failures; I believe there is a lesson, benefit, and blessing in all experiences, whether the outcomes are what we had hoped or something slightly unimagined.

What I have learned from Lisa during this season of ups and downs, wins and losses has forever changed the way I show up as a leader. This divine intersection going from a solopreneur to inviting in a co-founder has protected me from carrying the weight of the inevitable trials and tribulations when building a business from scratch and the harsh realities of raising money as a Black woman, scaling a team, maintaining strong financial rigor, and navigating uncontrollable outcomes.

I work on our relationship daily, clearing the scars from my previous co-founder relationships, being vulnerable and making a way for the goodness, mercy, and grace that is required when you are connected so deeply to another person who is interwoven in every aspect of your professional livelihood.

Co-founders will either make or break the company; according to surveys, one of the top three reasons companies fail is because of a disagreement or misalignment with their co-founders.

Lisa and I are bound by our interconnected character traits, our strong bias for action, true allyship, our commitment to do what is right. We will continue and leverage our individual gifts collectively to create pathways for success and progress. It is and will be greater than us, but our joint efforts will make an impact.

Find your allies, find your people, and hold each other close and accountable.

The Impact of Allyship

On my very first podcast to launch *Business of the Beat*, my long-time friend Nyakio Grieco, co-founder of Relevant: Your Skin Seen, Thirteen Lune, and Nyakio Beauty, spoke about the impact of allyship in building her second company. Upon writing this, BrainTrust Fund has become an investor in Thirteen Lune.

Kendra and Nyakio, March 2023, Los Angeles

"We speak about Allyship, here I am, a Black woman, a Black beauty founder, a first-generation American of Kenyan descent. Patrick (Herning) is a white, gay man. We really bonded over the fact that the only way that we are going to really be able to experience, from a business perspective, true unity, is to become allies of one another."

—Nyakio Grieco

Nyakio says inclusivity is something she and her co-founder were deeply passionate about long before the formation of Black Lives Matter and that they had come together really because of their passion for inclusivity.

Nyakio and Patrick launched Thirteen Lune in 2020 as the first of its kind e-commerce destination designed to inspire the discovery of beauty brands created by Black and Brown founders that resonate with people of all colors. Ninety percent of the brands carried are founded by Black, Indigenous, and People of Color (BIPOC), and 10% are ally brands.

Business of the Beat Excerpt, in Conversation with Nyakio Grieco

Season 1, Episode 1, December 12, 2020

edited for print

Listen on
Apple Podcasts

Business *of the beat*

WITH NYAKIO GRIECO
HOSTED BY KENDRA BRACKEN-FERGUSON

Nyakio: My beauty journey really kind of started when I was eight years old. I'm a first-generation American of Kenyan descent. I was born in New York. I was raised in Oklahoma. At the age of eight, my parents took me to Kenya for the first time to meet my grandparents.

My grandmother Nyakio was a Kenyan coffee farmer and a matron of a boarding school. She taught me my first beauty secret, using Kenyan coffee and sugarcane that she grew on her farm to exfoliate her skin. That's definitely when my beauty journey began. My grandfather, who was a medicine man, passed away before I got the chance to

(continued)

know him. He had the power to kind of go out in nature and extract oils to treat the skin and to treat many ailments. My whole life, growing up here in the States, my mom would apply these beauty traditions and these beauty recipes and rituals using oil on my hair, on my skin.

It's kind of all I ever knew were these powerful ingredients that come from the earth to treat the skin. While I was young, I wasn't necessarily always a fan of everything my mom wanted me to do. When it came to beauty, I really just fell in love with it. As I got older and kind of had this wisdom from my family, I also realized that the continent of Africa was very underrepresented here in the Western world, and I just wanted to be able to bring those timeless beauty secrets to everyone. And so I started my brand, Nyakio Beauty.

Kendra: It's so funny because in business school, when you think about your MVP, your most viable product, you spend so much time doing the market research, analysis, to determine what it's going to be. You were sitting right there with yours from birth, and it's so natural because you grew up seeing your family literally use it everyday. I love your story because it is so deeply personal and rooted in family, love, and the merging of cultures.

Nyakio: Yes, and even being the first-generation American, there's pride in that and history and heritage.

I was fortunate that I got to go spend time with my family in Kenya as a young girl. I only knew Africa to be this place that was sophisticated, so lush, so green, so beautiful. More importantly, people from this part of the world, from the cradle of civilization, had the healthiest glow, the most beautiful skin. I thought it was so crazy that here we are in America with access to everything and that people weren't celebrating Africa in that way. I started the brand, Nyakio Beauty, when I was 27. I was teaching myself how to be an entrepreneur, learning how to raise capital for the first time.

I don't have a science background. What I did have was just this plethora of knowledge and wisdom, and the proof is in the pudding—by looking at my best test market, my family and their beautiful skin and knowing that this stuff works well.

Kendra: I think that's really a good segue. I love how you talk about authenticity at the core and we can give the accolades for Nyakio Beauty. It's an amazing product. You're in Target, now. Congratulations!

Nyakio: Thank you. Thank you. God, that was a dream. Realized. Quite a journey, but so happy to be there.

Kendra: Alongside authenticity, knowledge, wisdom, and family, one of the things that we've also talked about was allyship and really understanding the benefits of allyship. I truly believe that there's nothing we can do in success that does not include the brain trust of allies that support and lift us up. I'm excited about your new venture that is literally launching right now, Thirteen Lune.

Nyakio: Thirteen Lune, yes. It's so exciting. Just as an entrepreneur, I often preach that entrepreneurs are not one-trick ponies. It's so exciting to be co-launching my next business, Thirteen Lune. *Lune* is *moon* in French and there are 13 moons in an astrological calendar. So I find the magic in that. Yeah, this company, Thirteen Lune, really is an inception of mine and my co-founder, Patrick Herning;

(continued)

he's also the founder of 11 Honoré, which is an inclusive sizing platform. Really, he was this pioneer that came to the market first with getting luxury brands to create sizing for women of all sizes. And he's had great success with that. Inclusivity is something he's deeply passionate about. It's something I'm deeply passionate about. Kind of long before this last pinnacle of the heightened moment that we've been living in with Black Lives Matter, we had come together really because of our passion for inclusivity.

We speak about allyship, here I am, a Black woman, a Black beauty founder, a first generation. Patrick is a white, gay man. We really bonded over the fact, and this is pre-2020, that the only way that we are going to really be able to experience from a business perspective, true unity is to become allies of one another. In discussing what does that look like in a business partnership, where do we find our strengths, where do we speak to our own authentic journeys and step into our purpose? I'll speak of myself, which is, I am a Black beauty founder, and I have been for almost two decades. While I am so grateful for all of the stops and starts and wins and challenges I've had in my life, one thing that I think didn't really hit me until I was in my forties is that, wow, this trajectory has been my trajectory, and it's been my journey, and I am grateful for every step of it.

A lot of the challenges that I face that I actually looked at as my own personal failures, maybe at times in my life may actually have had nothing to do with that. I mean, everything from challenges with finding retail distribution in my early days, challenges 100% with funding, and finding the capital to take my business to the next phase, and even challenges around it taking me until my forties to realize this. That like with many of my colleagues and allies in this business, having the idea, and I mean, my non-brown and Black allies and friends in the business, just having an idea opened doors for them where my doors are opened only after proving myself, only after getting to a certain number, etc. While a large part of that has to do with just being a woman, period, a great part of that has to do with being a Black woman.

I look at our industry in the space of beauty and all of the incredible talent that looks like me, women and men who have Black or brown skin and the fact that we are still such a small percentage of the opportunity. Of all of the things that I mentioned, that low percentage just doesn't make sense to me. What I realize is that my true purpose is really helping people who look like me get to success quicker and having the experiences that I've had. We move into 2020 and we've dealt with a lot of heartbreak. We've dealt with having to really look racism in the face in a way, especially within our industry, that we hadn't had to before.

The hopeful part of it is that there's the opportunity now to really listen. Thirteen Lune was born because I was just listening and Patrick was just listening over the course of the last six months. One thing that I realized is that with all of this incredible talent, all of these incredible brands, why is there not a contextual commerce platform where they all live? After George Floyd died, many of us Black founders were showing up on lists—top 20, top 50 Black-owned brands or Black-founded brands to buy. You would go to these articles, you would see all of our brands, and

(continued)

then you'd have to go to about 55 different sites in order to shop, right? Thirteen Lune was born of the fact that we wanted to create a place where we could amplify, celebrate, and curate some of the most incredible products created by Black and Brown founders because they deserve that spotlight.

Thirteen Lune is truly a place where allyship lives. Because without allyship and unity, none of us can win. In no business I believe, and I can say this with 100% certainty, no business that is coming to market or existing in market right now that does not have a plan to honor and celebrate unity and a plan to go beyond being multicultural—I say that with quotes to implement authentic celebration of all founders—is not set up for success. We wanted to create a space where we could not only honor and celebrate these Black and Brown founders and curate these incredible brands, but a place where our allies could also come and serve our customer as well.

Kendra: Without allyship and unity, no business can win. When you talk through the journey that you've had over 20 years as a Black business founder and to be female, and this notion that you look at other people who don't look like us, who can have an idea, who can get a seat at the table and walk out with checks, and that's not our reality. We have to prove ourselves, we always have. As far as we've come, we still have to overcome so much inherent bias and racism. The ability to say, and I love what you said, this is my passion, this is my purpose, and my purpose is to change the narrative for people who look like us to have a seat at the table, to create their own brands.

You talk about having a white male, gay co-founder. Even making that decision takes so much confidence in yourself to say that this person is going to be my ally, because it doesn't matter what they look like. What matters is that we are on a mission together to provide Black and Brown businesses a space to come together.

Nyakio: I've been in the beauty industry for almost 20 years and there's not too many of us. So I've had to find a way to navigate and find true allyship with other men and women in the space that don't look like me and to learn how to coexist and to appreciate and honor one another. And so I'm really excited for that. I'm also really excited for the Thirteen Lune.

I am so moved by Nyakio's story of her history, of her passion, and of her commitment to unifying the beauty industry. I stand in alignment with Nyakio, Patrick, and their commitment to standing in allyship and innovating the industry. Their commitment to representing the underrepresented is ever-present and a driving force of their success.

Who are your allies?

_____

_____

_____

_____

_____

What impact have they made in your life?

_____

_____

_____

_____

_____

12

In Closing

By June 2022, Lisa and I had made our first investment in the award-winning skincare brand BeautyStat, founded by cosmetic chemist Ron Robinson.

I met Ron on Clubhouse in 2020 when everyone was flocking to the social media channel to just talk and listen. We were in the same beauty groups and eventually found ourselves together every Tuesday morning on a standing call with other beauty executives and leaders sharing insights, being a support system, and more importantly just being in community as everyone grappled with the pandemic that had us all at a standstill. No one was immune, and we bonded over knowledge sharing.

Before we officially started raising our BrainTrust Fund, I ran into Ron at a gala in New York and we talked a bit about his fundraise, the growth of BeautyStat, and the direction he wanted to take the brand. I immediately knew I wanted this to be BrainTrust Fund's first investment. Initially Ron shared that he had closed his round (meaning he wasn't letting any more people invest money into the company), so I was pleasantly surprised when he called and said he wanted us in and made space for BrainTrust to join as investors. Within 72 hours of that call we made our first investment, and that deal set the tone for our future.

In season 2 of *Business of the Beat*, preinvestment, I talked to Ron about his early days as a chemist at Estée Lauder; his award-winning brand, BeautyStat; and his five-year journey that led him to unlock an untapped patented formula to develop his first Universal Vitamin C Skin Refiner. BeautyStat became the most googled beauty brand, due in part to this best-selling vitamin C serum, and it has been named one of the best by *O, The Oprah Magazine*; *Allure*; *Vogue*; and *Harper's Bazaar*.

Ron started BeautyStat after listening to consumers and using their feedback to go into the lab and develop a product based on true customer needs. Ron continues to stay patient and resilient in his journey to create BeautyStat. Since this podcast recording and upon writing this book, Ron has expanded BeautyStat across a larger retail footprint, raised venture capital, and continues to release and launch new products.

Business of the Beat Excerpt, in Conversation with Ron Robinson

Season 2, Episode 26, March 27, 2022

edited for print

Listen on Apple Podcasts

Business
of the beat

WITH RON ROBINSON
HOSTED BY KENDRA BRACKEN-FERGUSON

Ron: I'm so excited to be here today. I'm really excited to just get into it and share everything I can with you.

Kendra: I feel like I can always count on you to like my post on Instagram. Thank you, Ron.

Ron: That's what we're here for. That's what the community is about and happy to do that.

Kendra: Speaking of lifting each other up, I have to just start with Clubhouse because you are literally my Clubhouse mentor. You have truly taught me about the etiquette of Clubhouse and the importance of being active.

(continued)

It's its own mentorship and educational hub all wrapped in one audio soundbite.

Ron: Clubhouse is such a wild thing and I don't like to be on the phone and I don't want to speak on the phone, but yet I'm spending hours on my phone. How did that happen? It's funny, this platform, we're able to connect and share and it's all through audio and for some reason, people say, I found my place, if you will. I love the connection, I love the sharing, and it certainly gives an opportunity for all of us to connect with people that we might not have otherwise.

Kendra: It's so funny because I hadn't heard anyone say it that way and I feel the same way. I'm not a big talk on the phone person either. I think it's because so much of our week is spent on the phone in meetings that I just do not really want to get on the phone. It's so fascinating with Clubhouse and the community. It's broadened my world with all of the amazing beauty groups and the beauty clubs. It's very inclusive.

Ron: Absolutely. I've been in this beauty game for a long time and it's my pleasure to be able to share my experience with those new entrepreneurs that are looking for advice and tips. I often donate some of my time as a mentor to help connect with them, give them leads, introductions, and help them with ingredients and sourcing, etc. Again, it's been a great place for me not only to share what I'm up to and what I'm doing, but also to give back to those new entrepreneurs.

Kendra: I love that. Okay, I'm going to come back to the "mentor" piece you mention. Now, I want everyone to hear about your journey because it is just fascinating. I just imagine little baby Ron in a chemist uniform playing with potions. Now we have Ron, an award-wnning chemist and entrepreneur and it's just fascinating. So tell us everything.

Ron: It really starts with my mom, my parents, basically they're from the Caribbean. They moved to the United States in the late fifties. That was an era when parents really respected two real professions—a doctor or a lawyer. My parents had all boys, and we were coached to become doctors. Two of my brothers went to medical school, graduated, and became doctors. I didn't know what I wanted to do with my life. And I went to medical school. I hated it. I dropped out, moved back home with my parents, and started to send out resumes. I had chemistry and biology degrees, but didn't know what I wanted to do. Clinique, a division of Estée Lauder, called me in for an interview and I had no idea there was this whole world of science and chemistry behind cosmetics.

I went on the interview and they took me on a tour. They asked me questions about science, chemistry, and they hired me after a two-hour interview. That is how I fell into the industry. It became something that I really loved and was passionate about.

I want to go back to my mom because remember, I disappointed her by dropping out of medical school. That was her dream for all of her sons to become doctors. She was kind of heartbroken about the fact that I was going into cosmetics—until I was at Clinique for a few months. I brought home samples of some of the products that I was formulating. My mom was so thrilled and excited about getting beauty product samples from me and I was immediately

(continued)

forgiven. And then I was embraced. She embraced me in terms of me pursuing this new love that I found, and the new career path that I chose. It was that look in her eye when I gave her samples that drives me today. That really is what has driven me to this day. So that's where it started.

Kendra: I've had so many conversations with different founders and really figuring out the balance of what parents want for you and then finding the path of what you want for yourself. In some cases, and in your case, which is so beautiful, this kind of reconnecting with your mom on this level of I am successful, I did it my way, and her embrace and acceptance that powers you as a founder today.

Ron: That is really why I love beauty. Unlike other types of product categories, if I brought home food or pizza or cocktails, there's nothing quite like the experience of sharing beauty products with consumers or family members. It's like the most incredible feeling of joy. That's what drives me to develop great products, really products that people love and they really are passionate about and really delight in them. And that's carried me through my career.

I wanted to end the book with this podcast because Ron so eloquently connects my pillars through his own story of ambition and success. He starts with the importance of **community**, his commitment to **mentorship** as a means of giving back, and his ability to leverage his chemistry and biology **education** to create a career he had never imagined. While the podcast ends there, our story together continues through the BrainTrust Fund's investment of **capital** to support Ron's dreams of entrepreneurialism and building something that has never existed before.

All of the personal stories that I've shared in this book connect deeply to my purpose in life, and I am so grateful that the book is more than just my own narrative. My goal has been to bring you the collective wisdom, insights, and knowledge that can only be uncovered through community sharing. Writing this book and telling my story and the stories of my peers has been a true gift and one of the most enriching experiences I have ever had the good fortune of receiving.

It's amazing how in life things come together when you least expect it. I had talked to Charreah (featured in Chapter 8) about writing a book in 2018. I developed an outline and held it close to my heart. I often think of where I am now writing my story versus where I was back then—before COVID, before transitioning back into entrepreneurism, before developing several celebrity beauty and wellness brands, and before co-founding BeautyUnited, a nonprofit that was founded with a mission to mobilize the collective power and influence of the beauty and wellness industry as a force for good. My, how things can change in just five years if you stick to your beliefs, trust in your vision, and stay grounded in faith. In the past five years I also launched my podcast, *Business of the Beat*, that became the foundation for this book, built the largest platform dedicated to Black founders of beauty and wellness companies, and created my first fund that invests in the beauty, wellness, and consumer packaged goods space.

It is a blessing to recount my experiences. And I know that there is still so much ahead of me. What will the next five years hold? Maybe I'll catch you up in a sequel to this edition, but either way, it's a divine blessing to wake up every day and be passionate about life, family, work, and about the things I love. I hope sharing my story and the others in this book will help guide you on your own journey.

Reflecting on My Key Lessons

The following are some of my key lessons that I have learned along my journey. I have shared many with you throughout the discussion and interviews in this book, and I reiterate them here to remind you to pick out what you need from your experiences and let them guide you.

- *Carpe Diem: Seize the Day:* Life happens now. We are here now. Be in the moment now. Go for it. You can always pivot, go back, or take another direction. Carpe Diem has and continues to be my lifelong mantra.

- *Turn fear into faith:* I've lived both sides, as an intrapreneur and an entrepreneur, and had success through the psychologically challenging and rewarding times of both. At every turn I acknowledge my fear and turn it into faith.

- *God will humble you before He exalts you:* When you are humble, you can respond to and learn from criticism without becoming defensive—whether it is deserved or not deserved. Likewise, you can be aware of your failures without being emotionally devastated.

- *Create your own brain trust:* Find your people, stay connected, and build a trusted community to be a sounding board, help guide and support you in business and life, or even become your business partner.

- *Know your value and hold it:* Declare your value, own your value, and never diminish your beautifully unique gifts.

- *Walk with angels:* Let them lift and carry you when you need it and walk in the light together.

Thank you. Thank you for the gift of your friendship...and the gift of your belief in my talent. My gifts. Imposter syndrome is real for Black women...when we are the most maze bright people in many of these rooms. I won't ever stop supporting you and rooting for us.

Text message from one of my angels and friends, Farrah Louviere Cerf

Whether as an intrapraneur or entrepreneur, I hope that you will create a path that:

Rewards you financially

Puts you at its center or top

Affords you a future that is as bright as your talent(s)

Supports you as a person in your family and life

Surrounds you with good people who love and respect you

Connects you with powerful people who respect and advance you.

Excerpt from Julie Flanders' message, December 2017

I leave you, Dear Reader, with the gift of your own "homework" to expand your pillars, ignite your path, and help you navigate your own jungle gym of life.

What do you want most? Take 20 minutes to imagine yourself five years from now, laughing and bragging about your (future) current joy. Describe it here.

_____

_____

_____

_____

_____

I claim my nonnegotiables and I stand in my power as a Black woman changing the face of entrepreneurship, leading a community that will have a profound impact on driving and creating generational inheritance, investing in fellow founders, and building an ecosystem of winning.

I stand on my pillars:

Community
Mentorship
Education
Capital

I hope this book has been a source of inspiration, courage, and good fortune to you on your journey. I hope you have identified or expanded your own pillars and will continue to use them as a guide to create all the things you've ever dreamed of. Keep your brain trust close and keep putting one foot in front of the other. Celebrate your wins, both big and small, daily and stand in your power. May your life be greater and more fulfilled and your journey be grounded with purpose, full of hope and limitless joy.

Dear God, keep my eyes and ears open to receive Your blessings, to be prepared, to push forward with the gifts You have given me, and be grateful in all things; to receive abundance to speak my dreams and goals loudly and not be afraid to embody the truth. Success is within me, wealth is all around me, growth is abundant.

In the words of my mother, Teresa Bledsoe:

Love the Lord
Treat People Right
Do the Best You Can

Carpe Diem!

Acknowledgments

This book is inspired by my podcast, *Business of the Beat*, and all of the amazing entrepreneurs, intrapreneurs, influencers, and executives I have had the privilege of learning from and speaking with over the course of my career.

Business of the Beat continues to be solely focused on the business of beauty and wellness specifically from the viewpoint of BIPOC founders, senior executives, and operators. The podcast focuses on the real stories of passion to profit where guests share the highs and lows, successes and learnings of launching, building, scaling, and exiting their companies. It is these candid stories and direct conversations that inspired me to launch BrainTrust Founders Studio to provide an ecosystem toward winning for Black founders based on my own personal success pillars of community, mentorship, education, and capital. While my own personal journey was unique to me, many of the challenges, questions, and fears I faced were also shared with my fellow founders. Through these weekly recordings, I found my community of like-minded leaders who were willing to be transparent and vulnerable while also being mentors to the next generation by sharing their own knowledge and insight to help pave the way for others. Thank you to Celessa Baker, who first approached me about doing a podcast and introduced me to my network, Mean Ole Lion Media; our executive producer, Kenneth Johnson.

Special thank-you to each of the guests from seasons 1, 2, and 3 (through March 12, 2023). They are listed below, along with a favorite quote from their episode.

Season One

Episode 1

Nyakio Grieco, co-founder of Thirteen Lune

"While I am so grateful for all of the stops and starts and wins and challenges I've had in my life, one thing that I think didn't really hit me until I was in my forties is that, wow, this trajectory has been my trajectory, and it's been my journey, and I am grateful for every step of it."

Episode 2

Rea Ann Silva, founder of Beautyblender

"Beautyblender is a new tool for beauty and makeup, but as a professional makeup artist in the trenches, we are constantly experimenting with things. There have been handcut tools since the beginning of time."

Episode 3

Ella Gorgla, co-founder at 25 Black Women in Beauty

"I wanted to be completely honest and stand in my truth."

Episode 4

Micha Brown, celebrity hair stylist and owner of Press and Curl Bar

"Why would you go work for someone else for the same hard work you could be doing for yourself?"

Episode 5
Karen Young, founder of OUI the People
"We believe beauty shouldn't come at the expense of our psyche. Rather than pursuing flawlessness, we aim to build efficacious products, designed thoughtfully, that help you feel great in the skin you're already in."

Episode 6
Constance White, award-winning journalist, author, and former editor-in-chief of *Essence* magazine
"Invest in yourself. Know that you're worth it. If you don't feel it or know it, just act it."

Episode 7: Rachel Roff, founder of Urban Skin RX
"I have always been someone who's very empathetic, who hated seeing anybody not being treated equally."

Episode 8
Tina Chen Craig, co-founder of U Beauty
"I just knew what I wanted to do. I wanted to bring American businesses to Taiwan because it was a cash-rich little island. At that time in the '90s, it was the second holder of American dollars in the world. Powerful. Just talk about power-shoppers."

Episode 9
Charreah Jackson, executive coach and founder of Shine Army
"I'm not fearless, but what I am is courageous, and what I also am is clear."

Episode 10
Kim Seymour, chief human resources officer at Etsy
"I have so many examples of people who put themselves out there and poured into me for my development, both personally and professionally. What I knew is that I had the responsibility to make it two-way."

Episode 11
Diarrha N'Diaye, founder of Ami Colé

"Listen, I'm tired, it's not my fight. But then I realized, you know what, as tired as I am, 20 years from now can determine whether or not I feel comfortable where I walk in or less comfortable, so I have to be part of the solution."

Episode 12
Melissa Hibbert, founder of SHYFT Beauty

"If you have something you're interested in, don't delay it, just do it, otherwise you'll lose that momentum."

Episode 13
Tamerri Ater, founder of Gift of the Nile

"It's reciprocity—it was done for me and I want to be able to give it back."

Episode 14
Camara Aunique, founder of Camara Aunique Beauty

"I am who God has called me to be."

Episode 15
Dorion Renaud, founder of Buttah Skincare

"The key to being a successful CEO is letting others be great at their jobs."

Episode 16
Dametria Kinsley, vice president of global marketing at Cantu Beauty

"Make sure you have people around you that can check you."

Episode 17
Kimberly Radford Henderson, global vertical solutions marketing lead at Facebook

"We don't have all the answers and that's okay."

Episode 18
Lisa Price, founder of Carol's Daughter
"We have to get to a place where we celebrate the evolutions of business within our community. The beauty of being an entrepreneur is your ability to pivot."

Episode 19
Chidinma Asonye, COO at S by Serena
"Build a team for the future and not just where it is today."

Episode 20
Tekoa Hash, co-founder of The Teknique Agency
"I would go through that test again to get the growth from the downside, it built my confidence to get through it."

Episode 21
Shontay Lundy, founder of Black Girl Sunscreen
"This journey is not easy, it's more about the strength and confidence I have on a daily basis."

Episode 22
Tisha Thompson, founder of LYS Beauty
"When you get to a point where you have to reflect, what is your purpose, you get a sense of clarity."

Episode 23
Schenika Quattlebaum, founder of Natalia Me-gan
   Hair & Beauty
"Once I start something, I'm going to finish it."

Episode 24
Dr. Camille Howard-Verovic, founder of Girl+Hair
"Never let your accomplishments get ahead of you."

Episode 25
Lauren Napier, founder of Lauren Napier Beauty
"Bring people along with you, what people do with that information should be empowering to you and them."

Episode 26
Ron Robinson, founder of BeautyStat
"How will you be of service to others?"

Episode 27
Emeka Anyanwu, attorney and founder of A'me-kə
"Entrepreneurship is not for everyone, but I think it's important that everyone explores options to direct their own legacy and build generational wealth."

Episode 28
Daria Burke, advisor, board director, and investor
"Shoes may not change the world, but the women who wear them do."

Episode 29
Yannize Joshua, co-founder at The Teknique Group
"I had made millions for other people. So I knew how to do it. Now it was time to do it for myself."

Episode 30
Angela Stevens, award-winning hair stylist and founder of Conscious Curls Hair
"It was God's way of saying, you're not done here and people will respect you."

Episode 31
Dr. Nigma Talib, naturopathic doctor and founder of HealthyDoc
"You don't know how good you can feel until you do it."

Episode 32
Yve-Car Momperousse, co-founder of Kreyol Essence (KE)
  "It takes 10 years to become an overnight success."

Episode 33
Michela Wariebi, makeup artist, body painter, and
  entrepreneur
  "Makeup is where art and science meet."

Episode 34
Dorian Morris, founder of Undefined Beauty
  "I feel like everything happens for a reason, and it's this
beautiful mosiac of experiences that then leads you down
the next path."

Episode 35
Tai Beauchamp, co-founder of BROWN GIRL Jane
  "My focus is on changing the face of what wellness
means especially for Black and brown women."

Episode 36
Lucien Aymerick, founder of Charbon Plus
  "It's more than skincare, it's the whole reconstruction of
the Black self-esteem."

Episode 37
Brittany Scott, makeup artist and assistant boutique proprie-
  tor at Benefit Cosmetics
  "You're not (only) a makeup artist; you're a business!"

Episode 38
Kenya Eldridge, executive director of U.S. brand marketing
  at NARS Cosmetics
  "I moved to New York with only $300, but one million
worth of determination."

Episode 39

Jewel Bush, award-winning journalist and communications strategist

"For us [Black women] to be outdoors, and have a relationship to the outdoors that is rooted in leisure, pleasure, and not labor . . . is essentially a political act."

Episode 40

Amber Makupson, founder of Meraki Organics

"We have been left out of the conversation for a while when it comes to wellness, self-care, and even the health industry . . . so it's important for me to be a part of the conversation . . . of this transition in the world as a whole. I'm thankful and I'm doing my part."

Episode 41

Chaz Giles, founder of Revea

"We use technology to give consumers back the keys to their own body and to their own skin. We create a partnership with every consumer to help them optimize the things that are important to them. We start with the consumer."

Episode 42

Kim Lewis, co-founder of CURLMIX

"I want my customers to feel that they are creating value with every purchase they make. Crowdfunding allows my customers to earn shares of the company so that when they are buying Curlmix on their monthly subscription, they are also getting the equity."

Episode 43

Kelle Jacobs, founder of ASRI Wellness

"Just because it's done in this way doesn't mean it has to stay in this way. I am always looking at the world, what was going on in my life, what I was seeing as trends, and using that as an inspiration to develop new things and be an inno-vator."

Episode 44
Chinonye Akunne, founder of ILERA Apothecary

"Everything we have done with this brand has been very intentional from the minimalistic packaging, to the glass packaging, to our name. *Ilera* means 'health' in the Yoruba language in Nigeria. *Apothecary* is an old word for *pharmacy*. My dad's a pharmacist. My siblings and I grew up working in the family pharmacy."

Episode 45
Marcia Cole, co-founder of Fourth Phase Box

"If it feels right and you've grown yourself energetically enough, then go with it. You're not swimming against the stream, you're walking in the flow of grace."

Episode 46
Dionne Philips, luxury celebrity lash expert and founder of D'Lashes

"I'm a wife. I'm a friend. I'm a daughter. I'm a CEO. I'm the therapist. How do I balance it? Time management. I schedule everything, including my Peloton workouts . . . I make sure I'm keeping up with my time because time is my business."

Episode 47
Kameko Grant, founder of So Good General Store

"I was like . . . I'm just gonna have to start doing this on my own because I couldn't find that niche . . . I was looking for nontoxic, sustainable, no plastic . . . owned by a BIPOC member of that community."

Episode 48
Alisia Ford, founder of Glory Skincare
   "I was very intentional about the people we work with and the marketing as well because they all have life experiences that can add to the richness of what we are building in Glory."

Episode 49
Kitiya King, founder of Mischo Beauty
   "I cannot do it by myself. I will be the first to acknowledge where my zone of genius is and isn't and I've learned to speak up and ask for help."

Episode 50
Moj Mohdara, co-founder and co-chair @thebeautyunited;
   managing partner @kinshipventurespartner
   @intutioncapital
   "Getting older has come with a resolution of being comfortable with who I am and who I'm not . . . I know who I am. I'm clear about my values. I consider that such a privilege . . . these past 18 months have been brutal. I've had the time to push pause and invest in myself."

Season Two
Episode 1
Radha Kapoor, leader of venture partnerships at Clearco
   "The environment has improved for early-stage founders. When I was doing it, you were kind of out there on your own with zero support and very little in the way of resources . . . what is really great now is that there are accelerators and founder studios that are focused on specific verticals."

Episode 2

Jennifer Yen, founder of Purlisse and Yensa Beauty

"All these superfoods and I'm sitting here thinking, wow, this is amazing. At this point, I need more coverage on my skin, like a really great foundation. I want to take these superfood remedies, and I want to infuse them into color cosmetics . . . my ideas for beauty evolved because my needs were different."

Episode 3

Angel Cornelius, founder of Maison 276

"My mother actually discovered my first silver strand. I was so young and she was still combing my hair. So I've really grown up with this hair and understand the challenges of having silver hair . . . the challenge is how to keep your hair vibrant and colorful and bright without adding unwanted ingredients?"

Episode 4

Ezinne Iroanya-Adeoye, founder of SKNMUSE

"We have become very resourceful in making very intentional and calculated risks. We need capital that comes from people who understand what we are building."

Episode 5

Marquita Robinson Garcia, founder of DVINITI Skin Care

"The more we leverage technology and introduce different apps, different types of visual scanning . . . the more we are able to create a standardized process by which people personalize products and specific ingredients, the better off we will be."

Episode 6
Jordan Karim, founder of Florae & Noor

"I strongly believe that [if choosing a co-founder], it has to be an amazing relationship in which they understand you; they understand your brand, and where you want to go. And so right now, I'm solopreneuring it."

Episode 7
Rachel Lambo, part 1, co-founder of Sade Baron

"With this partnership, I got to see a layer other than Mom as a businessperson, a decision maker . . . my mom wasn't just my mom and a partner, but she was also my friend . . . I think that relationship is really magical, especially if we are working together on business and concept."

Episode 8
Rachel Lambo, part 2, co-founder of Sade Baron

"Discipline is very important when motivation is tired. It's a muscle you have to build."

Episode 9
Angela M. Davis, co-founder of AARMY

"I am somebody who has dedicated my life to living in purpose and to encouraging everyone else around me to do the same.

Episode 10
Dr. Natalie King, founder of Florae Beauty

"I think it's important to note with brands like ours. It's not just about giving a product; it's about how you make someone feel more confident in themselves [and] more confident in how they show up in the world."

Episode 11
Troy Alexander, founder of TROY Skincare
"I think for men, that's what we need to start doing. We need to start being better, getting stronger, and start loving ourselves."

Episode 12
Christina Tegbe, founder of 54 Thrones
"When I was a little girl, I would use it [shea butter] but I was always like 'why does our lotion come from Africa?' . . . as I got older I realized that was [my aunt's] way to make sure that I and my siblings grew up with part of our Nigerian heritage because we couldn't be physically there."

Episode 13
Helen Aboah, CEO at Urban Zen
"I knew after having [my daughter], by the way, that being a stay-at-home mom was not in my future. I knew that I want to be a mom but I also want to kill it in the business world."

Episode 14
Olivia Owens, Creator Partnerships at Teachable
"Timing is everything and when you try to force it, it doesn't materialize . . . Investors are looking for founders who know how to solve problems, not founders who have the answers to everything."

Episode 15
Leah Freeman-Haskin, founder of BLK OCEANS
"I do think that inner work is so important . . . trying to remove that self-doubt or at least having the confidence in yourself to know that you can pursue what you're passionate about and be successful."

Episode 16
Natasha Edwards, founder of THICK leave-in
"Community to me means the world. It would be my mission to reach out to the entire world and make sure they were able to have a THICK leave-in experience and also a wellness experience."

Episode 17
Saliah, Najiyyah, and Kareemah Mustafa, co-founders of Sabreen Cosmetics
"Our goal is to always create classic and timeless products that women can use for generations because they are so quality and also fit into their routine seamlessly."

Episode 18
Stephanie Bell, founder of Step Up & Glo'
"Being an entrepreneur on IG is different than being an entrepreneur in real life!"

Episode 19
Julie Napolitano, founder of Pup Wax
"If we stay in one place, then we limit ourselves and we limit the potential of what we can be and what we can build."

Episode 20
Akilah Releford, founder of Mary Louise Cosmetics
"It is important to be able to pivot and show agility as a founder, you have to be able to change constantly."

Episode 21
Abena Boamah, part 1, founder of Hanahana Beauty
"How do we make sure that we're not seeing Black people as a monolith? We're really looking at the global aspect of Blackness and how we in a brand can really grow."

Episode 22
Abena Boamah, part 2, founder of Hanahana Beauty

"I feel like as a child I understood that I was Ghanian. I understood that, yes, I was Black, too. African American to me was like yes, I am actually really African and I know where I am from and I am American."

Episode 23
Desiree Verdejo, founder of Hyper Skin

"You have to explain to retailers who you are and who your community is."

Episode 24
Chana Ginelle Ewing, founder of GEENIE

"You might have a great idea, but you have to be ready to match the moment!"

Episode 25
Junior Mintt, founder of Mintty Makeup

"I tried so long to be what everyone else wanted, and the thing that draws everybody to me is just being myself."

Episode 26
Kimberlee Alexandria-Day, founder of Ode to Self

"I just always wanted so desperately to have a skincare line because I wanted to see something out there for me!"

Episode 27
Tomara Watkins, founder of Loza Tam

"It has been a challenge just because the reality is that a lot of the investors tend to not look like you and they have their own single narrative of what is needed in the market and what isn't needed."

Episode 28
Hannah Diop, co-founder of Sienna Naturals
   "Performance is paramount!"

Episode 29
Ciara Imani May, co-founder of Rebundle
   "I had to find the right people to help me build the product of my dreams. I spent a lot of the time with the product team—I would never pretend to have the technical background to do this—but what I do bring is the vision and the direction that I want the product to go in."

Episode 30
Jasmine Lewis, founder of Vie Beauty
   "We're serving the community. We're changing skin day by day, and beautifying women still. Just moving forward, in whatever capacity that looks like."

Episode 31
Michelle Ranavat, founder of Ranavat
   "Being between two cultures is truly what inspired the brand! I'm so in love with the brand."

Episode 32
Brittney Ogike, founder of BEAUTYBEEZ
   "Beauty retail has failed women of color and I'm changing that."

Episode 34
Sherrel Sampson, founder of Canviiy
   "I want 100% formula ownership . . . I knew I had something special."

Episode 35
Dafina Smith, founder of Covet & Mane
   "The vision was there. The actualization of the vision was such a windy road."

Episode 36
Connie Lo, co-founder of Three Ships Beauty

"I'm a really big believer in manifestation and visualization. Part of it is speaking it into existence and telling people that you're interested. Speak it into existence."

Episode 37
Kimberly Smith, founder of Marjani Beauty

"I want to scale and grow bigger."

Episode 38
Jenn Harper, founder of Cheekbone Beauty Cosmetics

"Indigenous people are the OG's of sustainability . . . this is innately our culture: you are truly in relationship with every living thing."

Episode 39
Katini Yamaoka, founder of Katini Skin

"Once you put yourself mentally, physically in that space, the opportunity does arrive."

Episode 40
Brittany Golden, founder of IGL Nails

"I shifted my mindset that IGL Nails can create generational wealth for my family."

Episode 41
Joni Odum, President & CEO at Firstline Brands

"You fit the profile of a CEO, and I said 'okay, let's go!' My dad knew that I wanted to do it."

Episode 42
Youmie Francois part 1, founder of Flex-n-Fly

"When you have the heart of an immigrant and have a heart of ambition and want to rule the world like I do, you can take on assignments that you are not told to take on. I could not be anything but great."

Episode 43
Youmie Francois part 2, founder of Flex-n-Fly
"The best person I can be is me and do the assignment I was put here to do."

Episode 44
Carli Abram, founder of Pollynation Apothecary
"When you show up as a healer, you first have to heal very deeply your own self. These past few years have allowed me to heal deeply my own self."

Episode 45
Gracia Walker, co-founder of BROC SHOT
"Consumers should look at beauty from a wellness perspective and mindset. Look at the ingredients and understand the overall health benefits."

Episode 46
Maya Smith, founder of The Doux
"I am very clear on what I do, and where I excel."

Season Three
Episode 1
Monaé Everett, celebrity hairstylist, author, and founder of Texture Style Awards
"The way you make room is helping someone else so that there's room for you to receive what they're giving to you. If you're holding on to everything that you had, there's no room for getting something new. You're bigger, you're better."

Episode 2
Asha Coco, president of FORVR Mood
"Fragrance can completely change your mood. These fragrances are meant to change your mood and lift your vibe."

Episode 3
Denis Asamoah, co-founder of FORVR Mood
"There is a reason there is a team."

Episode 4
Arion Long, founder of FEMLY
"I didn't know the power of saying no and how it would free me. You'll thank yourself for the chance to set those boundaries later on."

Episode 4
Karen Lee, founder of GLOU Beauty
"Beauty is such an intrinsic part of our culture."

Episode 5
Tonya Lewis Lee, founder of Movita Organics; producer, director, and women's health advocate
"Never give up. Just at that moment when you're about to give up is when it happens."

Episode 6
Barbara Jacques, founder of JACQ'S
"When I started thinking bigger, I was able to put certain things in place. You have to be financially and mentally ready to enter retail. Sometimes we think we are ready but we aren't."

Episode 7
Olamide Olowe, founder of Topicals
"I've always had the intention of doing things that were hard, things that would help others."

Episode 8
Rebecca Allen, founder of Helix Hair Labs and Rebecca Allen, Inc.
"For me, I'm always trying to expand the conversation. And with hair tools, what is true, is that there's much more universality."

Episode 9
Kim Roxie, founder of LAMIK Beauty
"I worked seven days a week. I've helped thousands and thousands of women with their makeup and eyebrows. To then be upfront helping millions of people at one time was just a dream come true."

Episode 10
Anisa Telwar Kaicker, founder of Anisa International
"It is impossible to create a dream without believers in the dream."

Episode 11
Mahisha Dellinger, founder of CURLS
"The growth has been going on, but to say that you've made it . . . there's always more to be done, there's always more to do."

Episode 12
Daniel Hodgdon, co-founder of VEGAMOUR
"It's important we put love into everything we do."

Much gratitude to:

I also want to thank my brain trust, which continues to support and show up for me and my family. You have each played such an important role along my journey as a woman, wife, mother, daughter, and leader. Without you all, none of what I have accomplished would have happened in the way it did or when it did. For this I am thankful.

My family: Teresa Blesdoe (my mother and champion), Pleas Ferguson (my husband and best friend), Tierra Ferguson (my daughter), Mary Talley (my maternal grandmother), Donald Reese (my stepfather), Roberta Thompson (my godmother),

Kenneth Bracken (my father), Tony Bracken (my cousin), Brenda Glover (my mother-in-law), Tasha Reese (my stepsister), Quinton Shotwell aka SuperDopeQ (my cousin), Melody Ware (my cousin), Daphne Gordon (my aunt-in-law), and so many more relatives who have been there to lend a listening ear, make space for me to rest, write, and work and have been a constant source of support.

My long-standing executive coach, collaborator, and friend, Julie Flanders. Your influence is a guiding light for my professional journey and I am so thankful to bring some of the beauty from our sessions into the book. From our first lemon tree to the limitless boundaries of potential and abundance ahead of us, there is still so much to come.

Sir John Barnett, for capturing our first meeting and our intertwined entrepreneurial souls so beautifully. Thank you for taking time to pen such a thoughtful and dynamic Foreword to the book.

My closest friends and business colleagues, who have been rock-steady, supportive, a listening ear, and a shoulder to cry, laugh, and lean on. Whether for a reason, a season, or a lifetime, you have touched my life: Adrienne Alexander, DaVida Smith Baker, Johnel Baron, Julie Berman, Kristen Bright, Brandon Carter, Farrah Louvierre Cerf, Taia Cheng, Kathryn Finney, Mitzi Aimee Gonzalez Flor, Rachel Ghartey, Heidi Hovland, Mioshi Hill, Tussanee Lubbers, Moj Mahdara, Alan Rambam, Karen Robinovitz, Jessica Santoni, Ashli Sims, Tricey Wilks, Ebony Wilkins, and Julee Wilson.

To Katy Saintil, who I met when I was on the cusp of launching BrainTrust Founders Studio. Thank you for the late nights, daily texts, and copyediting on my early *Diary of a Founder* articles and for helping to put my thoughts onto paper for the foundation of this book. I remember our first in-person meeting on July 22, 2021, and the daily prayer that popped up on my phone after we said goodbye that said, "Father, I pray I would partner with others for purposeful connections and collaborations." At that moment, we knew we were going to work together.

My co-founder, chief investment officer, and fellow general partner, Lisa Stone, our advisory board for BrainTrust Founders Studio, and our investors in BrainTrust Fund, who have joined us on this journey of launching our first studio and building our first fund, protecting your names for privacy but you know who you are. A special thank-you to each and every founder who has joined our BrainTrust Founders Studio and helped us scale as the largest membership-based platform dedicated to Black founders of beauty and wellness companies and their commitment to support our work and give so freely to other founders.

Thank you to Kim Wimpsett, my editor, who stuck with me from beginning to end, editing and offering suggestions to make my words flow so cohesively. Victoria Savanh, my publisher, who emailed me on October 8, 2021, saying, "I've been following your inspiring work and wanted to see if you'd be interested in talking about a potential book project" and championing me and this project from beginning to end.

To all my fellow founders, I see you, I support you, I believe in YOU.

Carpe Diem,
KBF

About the Author

Kendra Bracken-Ferguson is an internationally acclaimed thought leader. In demand for her strategic vision and attention to brands that want to grow to scale quickly and sustainably, she is a sought-after speaker and C-suite/board-advising powerhouse.

Kendra's ecosystem of leadership is rooted in her global conglomerate BrainTrust, where she is the founder, CEO, and general partner.

BrainTrust is an award-winning, global marketing firm Kendra created in 2015. It was the first of her suite of BrainTrust enterprises leading to her founding BrainTrust Founders Studio in 2021, now the largest membership-based platform dedicated to Black founders of beauty and wellness companies that has not only changed the face of beauty but also empowered Black business owners to enter the room and sit at the tables of capital and wealth generation.

She is also the founder and general partner in the adjacent BrainTrust Fund, dedicated to investing in breakthrough Black-founded beauty and wellness brands. A transformative brand builder, Kendra is the secret ingredient in guiding and monetizing more than 200 influencer-driven brands that have collectively generated more than $100 million in revenue. Kendra has created and launched seven brands in partnership with celebrities and influencers. Among her firsts, Kendra has the distinction of being one of only 100 Black women ever to have raised more than $1 million in investment for her first company.

Not only has she innovated and partnered in the worlds of celebrity and influence, she has also been early to the power of technology and data to open new gates of opportunity as the youngest vice president at FleishmanHillard New York, the first director of digital media at Ralph Lauren, co-founder of Digital Brand Architects, the first chief digital officer at CAA-GBG (Creative Artists Agency—Global Brand Groups) when her company was acquired, and the co-founder and advisory board co-chair for BeautyUnited. She also co-developed Influencer

Data Mapping™, a proprietary advertising marketing solution to drive ROI (return on influence) and launched the Economic Advancement Report showcasing how Black beauty entrepreneurs are driving revenue, leading growth and taking shelf space.

Her list of awards and accolades is ever growing. In 2022, she was featured on the *Women's Wear Daily* 25 Most Inspirational Women List, was invited to join the Fashion Luxury Council at NYU Stern, and was featured in countless publications. In 2021, she was named to the *Glossy 50*: The Collective that Shaped the Beauty and Fashion Industry; named to Ulta Beauty's *MUSE 100*: A Celebration of 100 Inspirational Black Voices Making Beauty in Our World Possible; and was included in *LA Style*'s Most Influential List. In 2020, she was named as one of *Essence* magazine's "17 Inspiring Black Executives Redefining the Face of Beauty" and received the Purdue University College of Liberal Arts Emerging Voice Award. Kendra has been an invited speaker at some of the world's most innovative conferences: Harvard Business School Conference, SXSW, ShopTalk, CEO Summit, Advertising Week, Purdue Women's Leadership Conference, and many more.

As much as she does, she also gives. A noted philanthropist, mentor, and advisor, Kendra has received numerous accolades and funded an endowment at her alma mater, Purdue University, for a Black female student in the School of Liberal Arts.

Read more and view press clips and awards and honors at: kendrabracken-ferguson.com.

Index